MW00604658

The Luftwaffe Bombers'
Battle of Britain

Other Chris Goss titles available from Crécy Publishing

The Luftwaffe Fighters' Battle of Britain
The inside story: July-October 1940
Companion volume to *The Luftwaffe Bombers' Battle of Britain*

Bloody Biscay
The story of the Luftwaffe's only long range maritime fighter unit,
V *Gruppe/Kampfgeschwader* 40, and its adversaries 1942-1944

Brothers in Arms
An account of August-September 1940 through the deeds of two opposing
fighter units – 609 Squadron of the RAF and 1/JG53, a Luftwaffe *Staffel*
based in northern France

The Luftwaffe Bombers' Battle of Britain

The inside story: July-October 1940

Chris Goss

Crécy Publishing Limited

Published in 2000 by Crécy Publishing Limited
All rights reserved

A CIP record for this book is available from the British Library

ISBN 0 947554 82 3

Front cover
Main: *Oblt* Hermann Riedel (right) with *Fw* Willi Scholl of 8/KG 26, 1940 (Riedel)
top: Believed to be Ju 88 A-1, Werk Nummer 7092 coded 9K+MR of 7/KG 51 after its crash-
landing at Lille-Nord, 20 September 1940 (Hoehler).

Printed and bound by Redwood Books, Trowbridge

Crécy Publishing Limited
1a Ringway Trading Estate, Shadowmoss Road, Manchester M22 5LH

Contents

Acknowledgements

I have been writing to, and collecting accounts of, German pilots and their RAF opponents for the last twenty years. Sadly, many who have written to me over those years and whose accounts are contained within this book are no longer with us. To all of them I owe a great debt of thanks and only hope that I have managed to portray their life and death struggles in a fitting manner.

As usual there are a number of friends and acquaintances whose help has been gratefully received. I would therefore like to single out for thanks the following:

My good friends Mark Postlethwaite (for the proof reading, constructive criticism and encouragement), Bernd Rauchbach (for the translating and proof reading and continued help with research), Peter Cornwell, that mine of information on anything 'Battle of Britain', for his assistance with a number of photos and (Uncle) John Smith for giving me the original idea of this book.

The following all helped in one way or another – they are listed in no particular order:

Hans Hoehler, John Foreman, Bill Norman, Ian Hutton, the late Horst Grahl, Robert Ciuraj, Ken Watkins, Chris Fright, the late Siegfried Rauher, Rosemarie Wolff, Squadron Leader Philip Camp DFM, Mrs M. Morgan, Richard Wittmann, Andy Saunders, Len Gosman, Wilhelm Rosenbaum, Alfred Kull, Alwin Machalett, Erwin Moll, Jean Dillen, Kurt Miethner, Herbert Schick, Otto Blumers.

Finally, thanks again to my wife Sally and daughters Katherine, Megan and Alexandra. Time for a (well deserved?) break from book writing – at least for the time being!

Glossary and Abbreviations

AA	Anti-aircraft
Adj	Adjutant
Adler Angriff	Attack of Eagles – 13 August 1940 – also known as *Adler Tag* (Eagle Day)
Aufklaerungsgruppe (Aufkl.Gr)	Reconnaisance Wing
Beobachter (B)	Observer
Besatzung	Crew
Bf	Bayerische Flugzeugwerke (Messerschmitt aircraft prefix used by Germans)
Bordfunker (BF)	Radio operator
Bordmechaniker (BM) (or *Bordwart*)	Flight engineer
Bordschuetz (BS)	Air gunner
CO	Commanding Officer
Cpl	Corporal
Deflection	Aiming ahead of a target so that the bullets get there at the same time as the target
DFC	Distinguished Flying Cross
DFM	Distinguished Flying Medal
Ditch	Force-land in the sea
Do	Dornier
Erprobungsgruppe	Experimental Wing
Feldwebel (Fw)	Flight Sergeant
Fern	Long Range
Fg Off	Flying Officer
Flak	Anti-aircraft fire
Flieger (Flg)	Aircraftman
Fliegerkorps	Air Corps, subordinate to *Luftflotte*
Flt Lt	Flight Lieutenant
Flt Sgt	Flight Sergeant
Flt	Flight
Flugzeugfuehrer (F)	Pilot
Freie Jagd	Literally free hunting; fighter sweep
Fuehrer	Leader
Fuehrungsstab	Luftwaffe High Command Operations Staff
FW	Focke Wulf
Gefreiter (Gefr)	Leading Aircraftman

Generalfeldmarschall	Air Chief Marshal
Generalleutnant	Air Vice-Marshal
Geschwader (Gesch)	Group consisting of three *Gruppen*; commanded by a *Geschwader Kommodore (Gesch Komm)*
Gp	Group
GRT	Gross registered tonnage
Gruppe (Gr)	Wing consisting of three *Staffeln*; commanded by a *Gruppen Kommandeur (Gr Kdr). Gruppe* number denoted by Roman numerals (eg. II)
Hauptmann (Hptm)	Flight Lieutenant
He	Heinkel
Heckschuetz (HS)	Waist gunner
Heer (H)	Army
Hs	Henschel
Hund	Dog-slang for an aircraft flying as wingman to another (see *Kette*)
Ia	Operations Officer
Inj	Injured
Jagdgeschwader (JG)	Fighter Group
Ju	Junkers
Kampfgeschwader (KG)	Bomber Group
Kampfgruppe	Bomber Wing or formation
Kette	Three aircraft tactical formation similar to a vic
Kph	Kilometres per hour
Kuestenfliegergruppe (Kue.Fl.Gr)	Coastal Flying Wing
LAC	Leading Aircraftman
Lehrgeschwader (LG)	Technical Development Flying Group
Leutnant (Lt)	Pilot Officer
Leutnant zur See (Lt zS)	Sub Lieutenant
Lotfe	Optical bomb sight
Luftflotte	Air Fleet
Major (Maj)	Squadron Leader
Me	Messerschmitt (used by RAF)
Mit Eichenlaub	With Oakleaves (see *Ritterkreuz*)
NCO	Non-commissioned officer
NO	*Nachrichtenoffizier* – communications officer
Oberbefehlshaber der Luftwaffe (ObdL)	Commander in Chief of the Luftwaffe
Oberfeldwebel (Ofw)	Warrant Officer (WO)

Obergefreiter (Ogefr)	Senior Aircraftman
Oberleutnant (Oblt)	Flying Officer
Oberst	Group Captain
Oberstleutnant (Obstlt)	Wing Commander
Plt Off	Pilot Officer
POW	Prisoner of War
Regia Aeronautica	Italian Air Force
Reichsluftfahrt Ministerium	Air Ministry
Reichsmarschall	Marshal of the Air Force
Ritterkreuz	Knight's Cross
Seeloewe	Sealion – German code name for the invasion of Great Britain
Seenotflugkommando	Air Sea Rescue Detachment
Seenotstaffel	Air Sea Rescue Squadron
Sgt	Sergeant
Sonderfuehrer (Sd Fhr)	Rank given to war reporters
Sqn Ldr	Squadron Leader
Sqn	Squadron
Stab	Staff or Headquarters – formation in which *Gr Kdr* and *Gesch Komm* flew
Stabsfeldwebel (Stfw)	Senior Warrant Officer
Staffel (St)	Squadron (twelve aircraft); commanded by a *Staffel Kapitaen (St Kap)*. *Staffel* number denoted by Arabic numerals (eg. 2)
Stoerangriff	Nuisance attack
Stuka	Junkers 87
Sturzkampfgeschwader (StG)	Dive Bomber Group
TO	*Technischer Offizier* – Technical Officer
Uninj	Uninjured
Unteroffizier (Uffz)	Sergeant
Vector	A heading to fly
Vic	Three aircraft tactical formation used by RAF
W	Wounded
Walther PPK	Small pistol carried by German aircrew that usually fitted into a pocket
Werk Nummer (Wk Nr)	Serial number
Wg Cdr	Wing Commander
Z	*Zerstoerer* – destroyer
Zerstoerergeschwader (ZG)	Heavy fighter group
+	Killed

Introduction

Like many others, I have always been fascinated by stories of the Battle of Britain and how the outnumbered RAF fought and defeated a far superior enemy, namely the fighter and bomber aircraft of the *Luftwaffe*. For obvious reasons, accounts of what happened during the summer of 1940 tended to be centred around the defenders, be they in the air or on the ground. However, what started to interest me was the story of the Battle of Britain from the other side, a story that largely went untold – a fate always meted out to those who are on the losing side or team.

Twenty years ago, I started contacting those German aircrew who participated in the Battle of Britain, most of whom ended up being taken prisoners of war. At the same time, I attempted to trace where their aircraft crashed, who was responsible for their demise and, in some cases, put the victor and the vanquished in contact with each other. Over the years, a series of very personal, sometimes harrowing, sometimes heroic, sometimes tragic, stories have emerged which, when put in chronological order, give an interesting insight into the Battle of Britain from the antagonist's point of view. One must never lose sight of the fact that the *Luftwaffe* was an instrument of Adolf Hitler's evil designs for the world but, despite this, inside the German fighter and bomber aircraft (and for that matter, reconnaissance aircraft) were very ordinary people who had the misfortune to be born at the wrong time.

Do 17Zs of 7/KG 3.

The Luftwaffe Bombers' Battle of Britain is the sequel to *The Luftwaffe Fighters' Battle of Britain*, also published by Crécy. Both are the result of some twenty years of research which will hopefully allow the reader to see the Battle of Britain from a different perspective – in this case German bomber and reconnaissance aircrews' perspectives. The books are by no means a comprehensive and definitive story of the Battle of Britain but they will allow the reader to see what it felt like to be flying against a tenacious enemy who had nothing to lose and how it felt to be defeated when, for the previous year, all that the *Luftwaffe* had come up against was, in the main, a combination of disorganized, technically and numerically inferior opponents.

Prologue to the Battle

The invasion of Poland on 1 September 1939 saw the might of the *Luftwaffe* being thrown against a far more technically inferior, albeit tenacious, country. The *Luftwaffe* proved itself very quickly when its Heinkel 111 and Dornier 17 twin-engined bombers and Junkers 87 and Henschel 123 close support bombers, escorted by German fighters, all but achieved total air superiority in twelve hours. The speed with which all German forces, both ground and air, achieved objective after objective was astounding and just twenty-seven days later, the campaign was over and Adolf Hitler's intentions turned to the west.

The He 111.

Jubilant crews from 7/KG 3
– the date on the bomb on the right is 10/9/39.

The Do 17Z (5K+KR of 7/KG 3, 1939).

The Ju 87 B. (Grahl)

The Hs 123. (Grahl)

On 3 September 1939, Great Britain's Prime Minister, Neville Chamberlain, had announced that, because of Germany's unjustified attack on Poland, Great Britain was at war with Germany. France followed Britain's lead almost immediately and both countries geared up for war. It was not until 16 October 1939 that the first German bombers were observed off the British coast and then, that afternoon, fifteen Junkers 88s of I/KG 30 attempted to attack warships in the Firth of Forth. The Junkers 88 was the latest hope of the *Luftwaffe*, being faster and more manoeuvrable than the other German twin-engined bombers. However, a sharp lesson was learned when Spitfires of 602 and 603 Squadron intercepted, shooting down two and damaging a third. Both sides' learning processes continued for the next seven months with frequent but relatively small scale incidents and combats taking place.

The Ju 88. (Ciuraj)

German air activity was initially limited to the waters around the east coast of Great Britain with the Germans not wishing to commit the error of dropping bombs on the mainland and risking casualties to the civilian population (something the RAF was also trying to avoid doing over Germany). However, all would change on 9 April 1940 when German forces

Crews of 6/KG 4 at rest at Merville shortly before the 18 June 1940 mission. (Backhaus)

An early casualty – He 111 H-1 of 5/KG 26 was forced down by a Spitfire of 602 Sqn on 9 February 1940...

...Repaired, it flew again with the RAF.

invaded Scandinavia and then, on 10 May, did the same to France and the Low Countries. In each campaign, the *Luftwaffe* played a crucial part and by 4 June 1940, it was all but over. France gave in to the Germans on 22 June 1940 and the world held its breath. The only remaining opposition to Germany's aims came from Great Britain. Unusually, the first major attack against targets on the British mainland took place not by day but by night when, during the hours of darkness on 18 and 19 June 1940, Heinkel 111s of KG 4 lifted off from their new airfields of Merville and Lille–Roubaix in France and headed for airfields and industrial targets in eastern England:

Leutnant Erich Simon, *Stab*/KG 4

I had been assigned to bomb oil dumps near Southend. My primary task was to mark the target area by dropping flares. The underside of the *Geschwader's* aircraft would be prepared by applying black paint so that we would be less discernible against the dark sky. Unfortunately, this paint did not arrive in time and was not available for this mission.

At approximately 2230 hrs, I took off first, followed by the other aircraft at short intervals between each. Initially we headed north-east over the North Sea until approaching Denmark when we altered course to the west towards the target area.

As soon as we coasted in near Hull, we were spotted and tracked by searchlights but there was no sign or evidence of night fighters. Besides, until then, we had been told the British did not have night fighters! As planned, I dropped my flares on target and, after my primary task was accomplished, I continued to bomb selected targets which then caught fire. Upon completion, I turned on an easterly heading to get away from the target area and this is the last thing I can remember that night...

The RAF had thrown a mix of Spitfires and Blenheim fighters to try and get at the attackers. Unfortunately for the Germans, many of the RAF pilots in the air that night had recent combat experience:

Flight Lieutenant Adolph 'Sailor' Malan, 'A' Flight, 74 Squadron

During an air raid in the locality of Southend, various enemy aircraft were observed and held by searchlights for prolonged periods. On request from the Squadron, I was allowed to take off with a Spitfire. I climbed towards an enemy aircraft which was making for the coast and held in a searchlight at 8,000ft. I positioned myself astern and opened fire at 200 yards and closed to 50 yards with one burst. I observed bullets entering the enemy aircraft and had my windscreen covered in oil, broke off to the left and immediately below as enemy aircraft spiralled out of beam.[1] I climbed to 12,000ft towards another enemy aircraft held by a searchlight on a northerly course. I opened fire at 250 yards taking care not to overshoot this time. I gave five 2-second bursts and observed bullets entering all over the enemy aircraft with slight deflection as he was turning to port. Enemy aircraft emitted heavy smoke and I observed one parachute open very close. Enemy aircraft went down in a spiral dive. The searchlights and I followed him right down until he crashed in flames near Chelmsford.

'Sailor' Malan (left) seen here handing over command of the Biggin Hill Wing to Michael Robinson, July 1941.

[1] This aircraft was probably that of *Hptm* Hermann Prochnow, *Staffel Kapitaen* of 4/KG 4. His aircraft was observed going down at a 45 degree angle and on fire near the coast. Prochnow's body was washed ashore in July 1940.

Leutnant **Erich Simon**

Evidently I did bail out although I cannot remember doing so. Apparently I hit the stabiliser of the aircraft after I left the cockpit. The proof of this assumption was several broken ribs and bruises near my spine. In addition to those injuries, I had a bullet wound in my left arm.

The remains of Lt *Simon's He 111 – bullet holes in the tail are just visible.* (via Watkins)

During the bailing out, I lost my flying boots. I was in a state of shock when I landed but followed what I had been taught to "immediately leave the crash site or wherever you come down with your parachute". I cannot recall the direction or for how long I walked but it must have been quite some distance because my socks had completely worn away.

I next remember coming to the gateway of a farm where I passed out. The people were, considering the situation, friendly and the farmer took me to the Chelmsford and Essex Hospital...

As Erich Simon was landing by parachute, further north another combat was taking place:

Oberleutnant **Ulrich Jordan,** *Stab* **II/KG 4**

Stationed at Merville, twenty miles south-west of Flanders, our *Gruppe* had orders to bomb the airfields of Honington and Mildenhall, both known to be the bases from which bombers attacked Germany every night. On account of the skies over England being well guarded by day fighters, we decided to attack by night – about twelve aircraft out of twenty-seven from our *Gruppe*; the remainder were under repair following an attack by Blenheims the day before or the crews lacked night experience.

An He 111 of Stab II/KG 4.

Responsible for planning our attack, I phoned the officer commanding the fighter units in Holland, Belgium and northern France and asked him whether British night fighters should be taken into account that night. His answer: "Definitely not! We have no night fighters ourselves and I'm sure the British haven't either. Don't worry about meeting British fighters at night!" This was a mistake which led to a catastrophe for II/KG 4 *General Wever*.

On account of British night fighters not being expected, we decided to fly singly – one plane following its predecessors at ten to fifteen minute intervals, my plane being the first.

All went well up to passing the Thames between London and its mouth. Then, all of a sudden, about ten or fifteen searchlights started to search for the plane, without *Flak* firing. This was a hint to expect night fighters in spite of the *Oberst*'s "Definitely not!" After a few minutes, three or four searchlights caught my plane. Nothing happened – no gunfire or fighters. We continued on to the targets to the north east of London with one group of searchlights handing our plane onto the next.

Left to right Oblt *Ernst Dieter von Tellmann,* Oblt *Joachim von Arnim,* Maj *Erdmann (Gr Kdr),* Oblt *Ulrich Jordan.*

After a while, we saw far below, four points reflecting in the bright moonlight. A few minutes later, they were behind us – Blenheims. The fight lasted about ten to fifteen minutes. The fighters attacked continuously from the rear, one after the other causing a lot of damage to the fuselage, engines and the tail. The seats being protected by armoured plating are the reason for me being able to write this account even though they were not liked by the pilots, including myself, because of the extra weight. About a fifth of our Heinkel 111s had armoured seats and the plane I usually flew hadn't. By luck, I had to change to this plane because of the damage done to mine by the bombing attack by Blenheims.

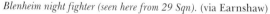

Blenheim night fighter (seen here from 29 Sqn). (via Earnshaw)

During the fight, the *Bordmechaniker* was hit twice – once in the belly and once in the leg so he was not able to use his machine gun in the lower part of the plane. The fighters, two of which had disappeared in the meantime (I don't know whether they were shot down or not[2]) now started to attack only from behind and below and finally managed to stop one of the engines at a height of 15,000ft about thirty-five miles from the coast. I then ordered the bombs to be dropped to make the plane lighter and to try and reach an airfield on the Continent. The fight continued until, eventually, the other engine stopped, apparently due to damage to the cooling system which happened just after the last of the fighters had disappeared, probably due to lack of fuel and ammunition...

Flight Lieutenant Raymond Duke-Wooley, Blue Section, 23 Squadron

Whilst flying at 5,000ft, three miles north of Kings Lynn, I observed an aircraft, subsequently identified as an He 111, held in a searchlight beam at 8,000ft. Time 0045 hrs. I observed a ball of fire which I took to be a Blenheim in flames breaking away from behind the tail of the enemy aircraft. I climbed to engage enemy aircraft and attacked from below the tail after the searchlight was no longer holding. Range 50 yards. Enemy aircraft returned fire and appeared to throttle back suddenly. Our own speed was 130 to 140 miles per hour and I estimated enemy aircraft slowing to 110 miles per hour. I delivered five attacks. Air Gunner [AC Derek Bell] fired seven short bursts at varying ranges. After a front attack, Air Gunner reported that the port engine of the enemy aircraft was on fire. I returned to base and landed as my starboard engine was unserviceable. Several bullets had holed the wings and fuselage of aircraft including hits in the starboard wing and the rear of the fuselage by cannon.

Oberleutnant Ulrich Jordan

...Now came the most important decision of the mission – to leave the plane by parachute or to try and reach the sea and land on its surface (landing on unknown land at night could have fatal consequences). Because my *Bordmechaniker* was severely wounded, it was impossible for him to bale out. Gliding, meanwhile, led to the

[2] Blenheim L1458/YP-S of 23 Squadron was hit by return fire and crashed at Terrington St Clement, Norfolk; the pilot Sgt Alan Close was killed but the gunner, LAC Lawrence Karasek, baled out uninjured.

decision to land in the sea close to land – I knew that a plane normally floats for a few minutes at least.

We ditched and left the floating plane, helping the *Bordmechaniker* out, and swam to the shore where we found a fishing boat which we used for protection against the cold, our clothes being soaked. After a while, men in civilian clothes with rifles, wearing a red badge on their sleeves, appeared. I went to them with my pistol in my hand and asked them in an urgent voice to get a doctor as soon as possible. They went away, probably glad that they hadn't any trouble, and after an hour, small groups of soldiers arrived, led by a First Lieutenant. They had a stretcher on which we carried our wounded crew member to a field station about two miles from the shore...

THIS AND PREVIOUS PAGE Oblt *Jordan's He111 lies just off the Norfolk coast.* (Humphreys)

As the two aircraft of 23 Squadron were battling with *Oblt* Jordan's Heinkel, further north, closer to the intended targets of Honington and Mildenhall, another Heinkel was receiving the attention of two different fighters:

Oberleutnant **Joachim von Arnim, 4/KG 4**

Oblt *Joachim von Arnim and* Fw *Willi Maier.* (von Arnim)

It was a full moon that night and, as far as I remember, no clouds whatsoever. Before crossing the coast en route to Mildenhall, we were easily found by many searchlights and unable to evade. On approaching our target, the rear gunner [*Fw* Karl] Hauck reported night fighters in sight. They immediately attacked us, hundreds of bullets hit our aircraft from the rear – it sounded like somebody hitting a thousand drums. Fortunately for us we had installed, just a day before, armour plating in the cockpit and for the two in the rear of the plane. The Spitfire made several attacks on us – it was funny to see the tracer going down in front of us. Both my boys in the rear answered the attacks with their machine guns. As far as I can remember, one of the

Spitfires was hit and shot down by my rear gunner at about the same time our Heinkel 111 went out of control – I always wondered if we did in fact shoot one of the Spitfires down…

There was more than one night fighter chasing after *Oblt* von Arnim and his crew:

Squadron Leader Joseph O'Brien, 'A' Flight Commander, 23 Squadron

…Intercepted one He 111 at 12,000ft in the vicinity of Newmarket. I opened fire at enemy aircraft with rear gun from a position below and in front. Enemy aircraft turned to port and slowed and I then gave him several long bursts with the front guns from 50 to 100 yards and saw clouds of smoke from his port engine. I then overshot enemy aircraft and passed very close below and in front of him. Air Gunner put a burst in at close range into the cockpit. Enemy aircraft disappeared, apparently out of control. Suddenly, I lost control of my aircraft which spun violently to the left. Failing to recover from the spin, I ordered my crew to bail out and I followed the Navigator out through the top hatch…

Sadly, Sqn Ldr O'Brien's Navigator and Air Gunner, Plt Off Cuthbert King-Clark and Cpl David Little, were both killed. Although the Blenheim crew were not aware of it, another night fighter was attacking the Heinkel and its pilot suffered at the hands of the Heinkel's gunners. Fg Off Petre was not able to file a combat report at the time but dictated the following to his Station Commander, Wg Cdr Woodhall:

Flying Officer G W 'John' Petre, 19 Squadron

Whilst on patrol between Ely and Newmarket, an enemy aircraft was sighted in the vicinity of Newmarket. Fg Off Petre shadowed it and was just about to open fire when he saw a Blenheim in the way. He then sheered off to one side and came in on the quarter of the enemy aircraft, firing a burst in a deflection shot. He saw his tracer going into the enemy and, immediately after, one engine poured out volumes of black smoke where the tracer was going into it. At this moment, our searchlights caught and held Fg Off Petre with the result that the enemy gunner had an illuminated target and opened fire. The Spitfire was hit by what was thought to be an explosive bullet and caught fire. The enemy aircraft immediately caught fire after and came down in flames near the Duxford–Newmarket road about one mile east of Six Mile Bottom. Fg Off Petre jumped by parachute after being badly burned around the face and hands…

Oberleutnant **Joachim von Arnim**

…Everything happened very quickly. [*Fw* Willi] Maier was unable to hold the plane on course and in a few seconds we all jumped out. In the moonlight, I could see I was hanging 200m above Maier. I saw the aircraft exploding on the ground and Maier and myself landed smoothly in a potato field. A couple of hours later we were taken prisoner by Home Guardsmen under the command of a Major Evans. He took us to his farm and then British soldiers took us to barracks at Bury St Edmunds. The next day, RAF officers ferried us to Duxford. They were all extremely polite, nice and friendly. Fine type of sportsmen. I was then told that Hauck had been found close to Duxford and had been wounded and taken to hospital. [*Fw*] Paul Gersch had sadly been killed when his parachute had failed to open.

Fw *Paul Gersch (left, with* Fw *Willi Maier), the only fatality in the von Arnim crew.* (von Arnim)

The remains of Oblt *von Arnim's He 111.* (via Watkins)

The remaining crew member Fw *Karl Hauck was wounded.* (Hauck)

This was not destined to be the last combat that night:

Unteroffizier Theo Kuehn, 6/KG 4

Uffz Theo Kuehn. (Kuehn)

We were flying at 5,000m altitude and had crossed the British coast south of Harwich. On the way home, the *Flak* stopped firing and a short time afterwards, I felt that our plane had been hit. The attack was a complete surprise – none of us saw the Spitfire. On the second and third attacks, both engines were damaged. I returned fire but without any result but to this day am thankful that we had armour plating. We flew lower and lower and when we were over Margate, the pilot started the right engine again so that we could ditch in the sea. At that moment *Fw* Alfred Reitzig, the *Beobachter*, baled out but got his parachute caught on the tail the same instant that we ditched.

We all managed to get out quickly and into our lifeboat. Of Reitzig, there was no sign…

Again, it was a Spitfire pilot that shot this Heinkel down:

Flying Officer Eric Ball, Green Section, 'B' Flight, 19 Squadron

At 0135 hrs, I had been detailed to intercept a bandit over Mildenhall at 12,000ft. At approximately 0150 hrs, I sighted the enemy aircraft which was held in a searchlight beam. As I was manoeuvring into position for the attack, it burst into flames and two occupants left the machine by parachute. I saw one machine crash about eight miles east of Duxford. I was then instructed to intercept a raid on Newmarket. I turned and spotted four searchlights concentrated on one spot roughly in that direction. After flying for five minutes, I saw the enemy aircraft which by that time had set a south-easterly course. It took me some time to overtake him and manoeuvre into position before I finally opened fire at a range of 200 yards, firing all the way up to 50 yards. I duly broke away and attacked him once more, experiencing no return fire and very little evasive tactics. By this time, the He 111 was enveloped in clouds of smoke and seemed to be losing height. As I broke away, the searchlights lost him and I consequently failed to pick him up again.

The crash of the Heinkel just off Margate would be one of many during the coming months and years but being one of the first, memories of its arrival are vivid:

Colin Cuthbert

We were on the cliff top looking out to sea when with a rush of wind, the He 111 came almost over our heads, missing a very large flagpole, over the cliffs and flopped into the water. We ran down a gap, split up by some 25 yards and very quickly dug two holes and pointed our .303s in the right direction.

A searchlight about a mile away clicked on and for the first time we saw the plane with water up to its wings with a big swastika on the tail. We really thought this was it! The Germans inflated their dinghy and paddled in silence to about 10 yards from the water's edge where they all put their hands up (still in silence) and sat there bobbing up and down.

I decided to show myself and shouted to Roy Ovenden to cover me. I waded in and pulled them to the shore. They got out and we searched them for weapons. They were all young and very cool, obviously thinking that they would only be prisoners for a short time. One of them combed his hair and a lot of jabbering went on – we couldn't understand German and they couldn't understand English.

One of them, after a time, put his hand on an under arm holster and handed in another gun. They then let us know that there was another crew member who had parachuted out. I then swam to the plane and found the missing crew member (dead) whose parachute had gone one side of the tail fin and he had gone the other. He had been strangled by the parachute cords.

And so ended the first major attack on mainland Britain during World War Two and what transpired to have been the first night combat of the war. The cost on the German side was six bombers (*Oblt* Falk Willis and his crew of *Stab* I/KG 4 crash-landed on the beach ten kilometres east of Calais after being damaged by a night fighter), nine experienced aircrew killed

Lt *Hansjuergen Backhaus, pilot of the He 111 that ditched off Margate.* (Backhaus)

Fw *Alfred Reitzig was killed when his parachute became entangled in the Heinkel's tail…* (Kuehn)

…he still lies buried in Margate's Cemetery. (via Fright)

Uffz Fritz Boeck, *another survivor from the Backhaus crew.* (Kuehn)

and eleven prisoners of war. Amongst those losses were one *Gruppen Kommandeur*, one *Staffel Kapitaen*, a *Geschwader Adjutant* and a *Gruppe Technischer Offizier*. RAF losses were four aircraft with five aircrew killed. The days that followed were quiet – a lull before the storm. Aircrew on both sides of the Channel needed a well earned rest to prepare for the coming onslaught. The combats fought on the night of 18/19 June 1940 taught both sides a salutary lesson. Even more lessons would be learned from the first day of the next month, a month which would see the start of the Battle of Britain.

The tail of Lt Backhaus' He 111 *is hauled ashore – the parachute of* Fw Reitzig *is seen near the base of the tail.* (via Watkins)

Officers of I/KG 4 just before the invasion of Poland – **Maj** *von Massenbach (second row, sixth from left) would be taken POW on 19 June 1940;* **Hptm** *Prochnow (back row, fourth from left) would be killed; most of the others would not survive the war.* (Koch)

The luckier officers of KG 4, all prisoners in Canada. **Oblt** *Jordan (front, second from left),* **Maj** *von Massenbach (front row, centre),* **Lt** *Backhaus (back row, far left),* **Oblt** *von Arnim (back row, third from left) and* **Lt** *Simon (back row, centre), all taken prisoner on 19 June 1940.* (Koch)

1
The Battle Begins
– July 1940

If the RAF was expecting an onslaught to coincide with the start of the month, they were wrong. Even though the Battle of Britain officially started on 10 July 1940, the month saw regular combats and incidents taking place off or over the British coast with each day seeing an increase in the ferocity and frequency of such actions. It was therefore ironic that the first *Luftwaffe* loss of July 1940 resulted in bitter recriminations:

The He 59, similar to that operated by Seenotflugkommando 3. (Rauher)

Leutnant **Hans-Joachim Fehske,** *Seenotflugkommando* **3**

Being a reserve officer, I initially belonged to *Kuestenfliegergruppe*
106 based at Norderney. After the Scandinavian Campaign, I was
transferred at short notice to *Seenotflugkommando* 3, together with my
crew, and we were posted to Amsterdam–Schiphol.

During the night of 30 June/1 July 1940, some German seaplanes
laid mines in the shipping lanes around Middlesborough. One aircraft
commanded by *LtzS* Schroeder had to carry out an emergency
landing in a British minefield off the east coast.

Our *Gruppenkommandeur* ordered us to fly to the area in question
and to look for this aircraft. The sea is large, a plane small, the speed
of the current very high because of the strong turn of the tide off the
east coast. My pilot had not been trained in instrument flying and that
was why we had to wait until first light for take off. Consequently,
another loss of time was unavoidable.

According to our dead reckonings, we arrived at the correct
latitude shortly before 0600 hrs. There we changed course and
headed towards the British east coast. My intention was to orientate
myself by finding a clear landmark. By doing this I would be able to
correct my position and improve the chances of a successful search.

During our approach, we were flying in low stratus/haze.
Immediately after changing course direction west, the fog lifted. The
visibility was excellent and we were flying between the coast and a
convoy headed south. One can understand that the RAF did not like
that. Consequently, there were two British fighters behind us a few
minutes later and very quickly we were shot down. Our plane was
painted white with big red crosses. According to international
agreements, we carried no armament on our search and rescue plane.

One engine and the light metal floats had been hit. The radio
equipment failed and our *Bordwart* received two gunshot wounds
(the bullets had passed right through). The floats failed to keep the
plane afloat so we took to our dinghy and tried to row towards
England. A short time after, we were fished out of the sea by the
escort vessel *Black Swan* and were taken prisoners of war. In
retrospect, I have to remark that we were treated remarkably
correctly and politely on board the *Black Swan*.

This was probably the first incident where an unarmed German aircraft
clearly on a mission of mercy had been attacked and shot down – the Red
Cross markings must have been clearly visible to the three 72 Squadron pilots
responsible even though one of the combat reports makes little mention:

Flight Sergeant Harry Steere, Blue 3, 72 Squadron

Blue 1 [Flt Lt Ted Graham] ordered Number One attack. Blue 1 and 2 [Fg Off Edgar Wilcox] fired, I closed to 250 yards and the machine turned right. I had a simple deflection shot. The machine touched the water and I broke off the attack. The machine jettisoned several articles after Blue 2 finished his attack.

Pilots of 72 Sqn at readiness at Acklington, July 1940. (Pocock)

Despite German complaints, the three RAF pilots' actions were vindicated when an order was issued that any German plane, armed or otherwise, found in the vicinity of a British convoy did so at their own risk.

Sporadic combats and incidents continued throughout the day but, just before tea-time, the RAF fighters in the north claimed another victim:

Oberleutnant Friedrich-Wilhelm Koch, 3/KG 4

On 1 July 1940, my *Gruppe* was for the first time ordered to perform a daylight attack against an industrial target. Each of the three *Staffel* had to nominate one crew – in my *Staffel*, I volunteered and was lucky to get the last serviceable aircraft. However, that aircraft, unfortunately, also became unserviceable during pre-take off checks but the indefatigable groundcrew managed to allow me to take off two hours later.

Oblt *Friedrich-Wilhelm Koch, Copenhagen, April 1940.* (Koch)

We were to undertake a high level attack against a chemical works at Middlesborough with a secondary target being the oil tanks at Hull. So, with the Juist Beacon as a navigational aid, the course was set for Flamborough Head. The weather conditions for the attack (attack was to be broken off if the cloud cover 100 kilometres from the coast was less than 5/10ths) did not suit. However, after hearing that both the other aircraft had broken off their attacks, I felt obliged to press home my attack. Just short of 100 kilometres from the coast, a thin stratus layer indicated that cloud cover could be expected. At about 1630 hrs (German Summer Time), we descended, and broke through clouds exactly where we wanted to be – just south of Flamborough Head. However, I decided not to fly to Middlesborough but to turn south where the cloud cover seemed to be thicker.

He 111 of 3/KG 4, Langenau, September 1939. (Koch)

Just north of the Humber Estuary, the cloud broke up and the town of Hull lay in front of us under a nearly spotless blue sky. Shortly afterwards having left the cloud cover, my *Bordfunker* [*Fw* Alfred Weber] reported three Spitfires. In order not to be spotted by them, I turned back into cloud and headed towards Middlesborough. After twenty minutes, the cloud broke up and became thin and hazy. Whilst I was pondering on what to do, again Spitfires were reported in sight. Six of them flying at the same altitude but apparently not having sighted us. It seemed to me that it was more than mere chance that these fighters were there and only afterwards did I learn about radar. My ignorance of radar resulted in me deciding to fly eastwards for ten minutes then, at a safe distance parallel to the coast up to Hull.

I intended remaining in cloud and then to break cloud to orientate myself for the subsequent attack. This was our last chance as apart from being low on fuel, my pilot [*Ofw* Hermann Draisbach] had only twenty minutes oxygen remaining due to a defect in the oxygen system. Navigation was exact as when leaving cloud, we hit the coastline. Suddenly I saw an airfield with a number of light coloured planes. In a sudden impulse, I felt tempted to attack this dream target. However, the lack of the usual camouflage led me to think that it was a mock airfield and I resisted the temptation.

Ofw *Hermann Draisbach (right) and* Ofw *Rudolf Ernst.* (Koch)

We were now in cloud at about 18,000ft. Some scattered clouds at about 12,000ft obscured my view so we descended. Shortly before reaching the town, I turned in for the final run when my *Bordfunker* again reported three Spitfires in sight. I had to make a quick decision – either to return into the cloud or to continue the target run. Since it was doubtful that we would make it home, I decided to do what I was here for – to bomb the oil tanks. For the whole time we were in the target area, we were subjected to *Flak* which was extremely unpleasant during the final approach because for best results, I had to keep altitude, speed and course constant thus giving the gunners an easy target. In fact, one of the shell fragments entered the cockpit and damaged part of the instrument panel.

In spite of these irritations, we continued the target run up to the moment I dropped the bombs. I must say I have praise for the outstanding performance of my pilot who executed my corrections with calmness and coolness. After I dropped my bombs, I ordered the pilot to perform a steep turn and to dive at full speed. I noticed that the twelve 50 kilogram bombs had straddled the target with several hits, causing explosions and fire. I tried to set up a coded mission report because I doubted very much that we could do it later.

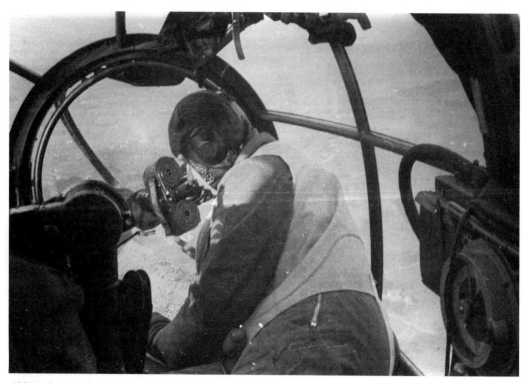

Oblt Koch in position in the He 111. (Koch)

Still several thousand feet up, we reached the Humber Estuary when the Spitfires circled in for their first attack. For the time we flew in the *Flak* zone, they had waited a safe distance but now they closed for the kill. Although lying in the front part of the plane, manning the forward gun, I was able to follow the events over the intercom...

Pilot Officer John Brewster, Yellow 3, 616 Squadron

I followed Number 2 [Plt Off John Bell] into the attack. On going into the attack, I noticed that the port engine was on fire and a little smoke appeared from the starboard engine. Fire was opened at about 220 yards and tracer bullets were seen to go into the fuselage and wings. A lot of debris fell off from the enemy aircraft approximately halfway up the fuselage on the top port side. Range was now about 100 yards. Oil then appeared on my windscreen and when closing to about 50 yards, enemy aircraft was completely enveloped in a circular cloud of black smoke. My windscreen was now completely covered in oil and it was impossible to distinguish enemy aircraft in the smoke. I broke right because I was very near the enemy aircraft and it seemed better to break right than left where Number 2 had broken. I then turned east at about 4,000ft and saw enemy aircraft below me diving down to the sea on fire. I manoeuvred to attack again and on turning dead astern of the enemy aircraft in a diving turn, I lost sight of it due to the oil on my windscreen. I had dived to 2,000ft and then turned to starboard and circled for enemy aircraft but failed to locate it. I then returned to base and landed.

Tracer ammunition was most useful and enabled me to see where my bullets were hitting enemy aircraft. No enemy fire was encountered. On landing, I found that there were three dents in my wing caused by flying debris from enemy aircraft. Also, the leading edge of my mainplane, especially the port, spinner, wireless aerial mast, tailplane leading edge and fin were covered with a film of oil in addition to the windscreen through which it was impossible to see for landing, necessitating looking over the side.

Oberleutnant Friedrich-Wilhelm Koch

...Already after the first machine gun bursts of my *Bordfunker* in the upper rear position, the gun had suffered a malfunction. From this moment on, the Spitfires could perform their attacks unhindered and from close range. One after the other made his run. Each time a Spitfire launched his attack, a noisy stream of bullets rushed through our aircraft. At first the instrument panel was shot to pieces, then one engine put out of action. Next, the landing gear came down and the flaps flew off. After the second engine was also put out of action and the starboard ailerons had been shot away, the Spitfires left their crippled victim and returned to their base. The pilot, without instruments, flaps and ailerons, a damaged rudder and propellers that could not be feathered, struggled with the controls, miraculously keeping the aircraft flying. Now after the continuous rattling noise of the bullets had stopped, it became dead and quiet in the aircraft. My pilot asked me to guess the speed and altitude since he had no instruments and was fully occupied in struggling with the controls.

The exposed pilot's instrument panel in the He 111. (Backhaus)

I called the *Bordmechaniker* [*Ofw* Rudolf Ernst] who answered that the *Bordfunker* had been hit several times and it seemed likely that he was dead. He himself had been hit in the leg and buttocks and was joking about an inglorious end! I went back, noticed that we could not get out the dinghy there because the dead *Bordfunker* blocked the upper exit so I pulled the dinghy into the cockpit, followed by the *Bordmechaniker*. Back in the cockpit I realised that we were very low over the surface of the sea and I could assist the pilot by calling out the distance to the surface until we hit. Due to the undercarriage being down, we flipped over and started sinking. Because of the impact, I was thrown forward

Oblt Koch (right) and his crew practice inflating the dinghy – this practice helped on 1 July 1940. (Koch)

and lost consciousness. Then, when I had recovered, I noticed that we were under the water and that water was streaming through many openings. However, we all floated upwards and broke surface, floating silently. We brought our dinghy over, inflated it and our lifebelts and got on board the dinghy. At this moment, we saw the *Bordfunker* move so we got the dinghy to him and pulled our badly wounded comrade on board. At the same moment, the Heinkel sank.

Now for the first time we were in a position to analyse our new situation. In view of the critical state of the *Bordfunker* who had been shot through the eye, head, an arm and chest, we decided to use signal flares and markers to signal our position to a Short Sunderland flying boat which had been circling over the convoy we had seen from the air. Since we were about 25 miles off the British coast, we could not hope for rescue by German vessels, at least not during the night to come. About half an hour later, a ship came in sight (the *Black Swan*) and we were taken on board...

After such a frantic start to the month, the poor weather hampered air operations on 2 July with just one combat resulting in one German loss (a reconnaissance aircraft) on that day. The return of the good weather saw the air activity increase over the following days but with no real obvious pattern. However, the appearance of the much feared *Stuka* over Portland Naval base on the morning of 4 July was a portent of things to come, or was it? The absence of RAF fighters over the German's target allowed them to get away scot-free (and resulted in the award of the Victoria Cross to anti-aircraft gunner Jack Mantle). The same day also saw the first concerted attack on shipping when eighteen Dornier 17s of II/KG 2 attacked a small convoy off the straits of Dover in the mid-afternoon. The escort of thirty Messerschmitt 109s kept two squadrons of RAF fighters away and just two of the German bombers returned with lightly wounded crew members.

It was not until 7 July that there was a marked increase along the length and breadth of Great Britain but with the main effort again being against a convoy sailing from west to east along the Channel. It must have been clear to the RAF that convoys were the *Luftwaffe*'s chosen prey and on this day RAF casualties had been high (seven fighters lost and four pilots killed) whilst no bombers had been lost in the convoy attack.

Experienced pilot Fw Richard Saft and his crew of 2/KG 77 were lost on 3 July 1940; briefed to strafe the area in between Dover and Hawkinge, it is thought they were shot down by ground fire and crashed into the Channel. (Bohn)

Another success – what is believed to be the sinking of the Kolga *by Uffz Robert Ciuraj, 4/KG 51 on 4 July 1940.* (Ciuraj)

Uffz *Ciuraj and his crew of 4/KG 51.* (Ciuraj)

The Do 17 of Ofw *Hans Wolff of KG 2 (second from right, seen as a POW in Canada later in the war) was damaged in combat off Dover on 4 July 1940; coincidentally the officer to his right,* Hptm *Alfred Kindler, collected him by car from where he landed later that day.* (Wolff)

The day after was not much better with the *Kanalkampffuehrer* (literally Channel Bomber Leader) *Oberst* Johannes Fink's Dornier 17s having another go at another convoy. The scene was setting fast.

The Dornier 17s of III/KG 2 continued where they had left off by attacking convoy BREAD on the afternoon of 10 July 1940. The day after, it was the turn of yet another convoy and the harbours of Portland and Portsmouth (the former receiving the attention of *Stukas*, the latter Heinkel 111s). The latter attack could have been partly responsible for what happened the following afternoon. The Heinkel 111s of KG 55 had been tasked on this daylight raid and were also to attack Cardiff by night on 12 July and one of the *Geschwader*'s Heinkels had been sent out to have a look:

Feldwebel Heinz Kalina, *Stab*/KG 55

We started around midday from Villacoublay near Paris for a reconnaissance flight over southern England. The weather was fine. Suddenly, near Portsmouth at about 6,000m altitude, we were attacked by about a dozen Hurricanes and we were badly hit. The starboard engine cut out and we had to land. Badly wounded, we were taken prisoner.

Sitting duck – the Stab/KG 55 *He 111 shot down on 12 July 1940.*

Heinz Kalina's account does not reveal the carnage that the Hurricanes of 43 Squadron must have inflicted on this lone, relatively undefended German bomber. For those RAF pilots involved, it must have been a simple 'kill'. However, an eyewitness on the ground gives a better idea as to what happened:

Alexander McKee

With one engine spluttering and banging, it came towards a field near the village of Southwick; wheels up, it passed over a hedge and went skidding and bumping wildly across a ploughed field coming to a stop 50 yards from a public house... The observer, shot through the head, lay dead across the bombsight. A subaltern from one of the forts on Portsdown Hill took the surrender of the crew about an hour after they had come down – owing to the winding country lanes, it took some time to find the crash[1]

The Heinkel was painted grey and green on top, light greenish blue below; the *Geschwader* crest was a red griffon with blue wings on a shield...

I crawled in through a small hatch on the port side and walked up to the nose... I settled down in the pilot's seat and tried out the controls and then had a look at the instrument panel: a gyro, larger than ours, artificial horizon, Lorenz indicator for blind flying with kicker and one neon light only and most interesting of all, a vertical compass with no grid wires or north seeking needle. Instead a miniature aeroplane pointing the bearing...

I got into the front gunner's position – the nose was entirely perspex, now rather blood-spattered. There was a trap door in the floor where he lay when firing the gun. I slid back the trap door revealing a blood-drenched bombsight and compass. The blood must have pumped out – every cranny was thickly saturated with it...

Convoy attacks continued on 13 and 14 July when the RAF suffered at the hands of the escorting German single-engined fighters. It was a different matter when the German bombers were escorted by just the twin-engined Messerschmitt 110s.

Poor weather had again made itself felt on 14 July and for the next four days German bombers did stray over and around Great Britain but for a number of crews, the bad weather did not protect them:

Oberleutnant Ottmar Hollman, 2/KG 26

On 15 July 1940, I started out on my mission at about 1000 hrs from Kristiansand, Norway. The sky was blue until I reached the middle of the North Sea. Then there was an unbroken layer of cloud beneath me. I was flying at about 2,000m; the wind was from the south-west.

I had calculated that shortly before the British coast, I should

---

[1] The dazed German crew were captured by 37 year-old Samuel Brown and the landlord of the 'Horse and Jockey' public house with the aid of a toy pistol. Interest in the crash and the exploits of the captors resulted in many visitors and "a fortnight's supply of beer [was] sold in just one night".

descend through the cloud
and orientate myself. I came
out of the cloud at 200m or
300m and at first saw only
the sea below me. After a
short time, however, I
reached the coast. Here the
cloud was solid and was only
100m up. It was very difficult
to fix one's position. My
Beobachter [*Uffz* Erich Walz]
made out that we were north
of our target. The target was
an airfield just north of the
Firth of Forth where night
fighters were reported to
have been based[2]. So, I flew

The North Sea as seen from the cockpit of a KG 26 He 111. (Zimmer)

southwards and the cloud base got lower and lower and I was just
above sea level. I can still remember quite clearly that there was a
lighthouse on my right hand side and I felt that I could reach out and
touch it. Soon, however, we
could see absolutely nothing as
the clouds came down to sea
level. I was forced to abandon
this approach. I pulled up into
the clouds and took a course for
the secondary target –
Aberdeen Harbour. But here
too, I saw nothing because of
the covering clouds and mist. I
began to consider whether I
should at once return to
Kristiansand or to try once
again to reach the airfield. I
took the latter course and flew

Oblt *Hollmann (front centre)*. (Hollmann)

south into the clouds, hoping for better visibility as the wind was
coming from the south west and that I could get a visual fix and reach
the target that way.

At the time, I was well aware that my flight was being tracked by
British ground stations and that with an improvement in the weather,
I would have to reckon with Spitfires. The weather gave me a feeling

---

[2] With an increase in night missions, the *Luftwaffe* had already learned what effect
a potent night fighter force could have. However, their intelligence was not good –
no night fighter base existed.

of security – after an attack, I could vanish back into the clouds.

Then, suddenly, the clouds became a little thinner and the cloud base rose to about 100m. I climbed in order to fly immediately below the clouds so that if in danger of attack, I could vanish. However, it was already too late because the next second, two Spitfires attacked...

Pilot Officer James Morton, Yellow Section, 'A' Flight, 603 Squadron

I think that he was very unlucky to get downed as we only had quite a short burst each with quite a lot of deflection. I think that it was almost certainly Dudley [Plt Off Dudley Stewart-Clarke] who did the damage though it could have possibly been me who hit his port engine as I remember thinking at the time that I had made rather a cock of it and missed him to port. I take it that it was the rear gunner who was killed – they seemed to have very little protection which was just as well as some of them were very good shots. I got a lot of bullet holes a few days later from another Heinkel 111 and was extremely lucky to get home.

Oberleutnant Ottmar Hollman

...My starboard engine was hit and the starboard wing was riddled with hundreds of holes, one man dead and another wounded in the upper part of the thigh. The radio was wrecked. My immediate and instinctive reaction was a sharp turn to port in order to vanish into the clouds again. I then saw two Spitfires fly past.

This all happened in a few seconds and then I was back into the clouds. First we jettisoned our bombs. I switched off the starboard engine and successfully feathered the propeller. Thick plumes of smoke came out of the engine and the oil temperature rose to the point of the engine seizing.

My port engine was running quite normally and all instrument indications were normal. I was flying on instruments on just the port engine and intended to return to Kristiansand. I had all the dead weight such as the guns thrown out and tried to gain height. After twenty minutes I succeeded in getting to 800m. Even I was convinced I could reach Norway. Then it happened – the port engine failed! I immediately put the nose down to gain speed – over the intercom, I told the crew we were ditching. I came out of the cloud at 100m and saw below me the white caps of the restless sea. I then landed wheels up in the water. I tried to touch down tail first – I succeeded and set the aircraft down with a great deal of noise. For a split second, I could see nothing but the water around me and I thought this was the end. The cockpit and I then surfaced again. I opened the upper window and climbed out. I ran back over the fuselage in order to help my crew out. I got them and the dinghy out at the rear – there were four of us as the dead man [*Ogefr* Walter Reinhardt] remained in the plane. The dinghy was successfully inflated by a compressed air bottle – fortunately it was undamaged (even today, I'm still grateful to the two British pilots for that!).

We had barely got into the dinghy when the He 111 put its nose down and vanished into the sea, the tail nearly taking us with it. It was suddenly very quiet. We bobbed up and down in isolation on the waves, up to our navels in water. We had three paddles at our disposal and I told my crew that I didn't think we could reach Norway but we could reach the British coast if we put all our strength into it.

We finally landed two or three days later. I cannot remember where exactly. We had sighted land then were picked up in a state of total exhaustion by two friendly Scottish fishermen about a mile off shore. I calculated that we had crashed into the sea 50 to 80 kilometres off the coast. By our own efforts, but also I suspect as a result of a particularly favourable current, we were driven far to the north. The days spent in the dinghy, the spiritual, mental and physical events and experiences are a different story...

The RAF Dyce Station Record Book noted they were landed at Fraserburgh on 17 July and had spent fifty hours at sea, attributing their survival to regular dinghy and ditching practice back in Norway!

The bad weather continued for the next two days with only isolated or sporadic attacks occurring. An improvement on 18 July allowed the *Luftwaffe* to increase the number of reconnaissance flights and incursions by lone bombers. However, on 19 July the weather improved sufficiently for an attack by *Stukas* against Portland and Dover and, curiously, Heinkel 115 seaplanes to lay mines in the Thames Estuary. RAF losses outweighed *Luftwaffe* losses on this day, not helped by the massacre of 141 Squadron's Boulton Paul Defiants by Messerschmitt 109s of III/JG 51.

On the night of 19/20 July, an unusual loss occurred when a Focke Wulf 200 *Condor* was shot down by anti-aircraft guns off Hartlepool. The *Luftwaffe* had felt confident enough to commit one of its four-engined bombers to mine-laying tasks close to the British Coast but this loss and another, lost a few days later, would cause them to change their tactics and to commit the vulnerable *Condor* to missions further away from enemy territory.

20 July saw a number of combats and German incursions which included the shooting down of two more Heinkel 59 seaplanes and an attack on another convoy which resulted in the RAF fighters successfully bouncing the German formation from out of the sun. For the RAF, the day was a vast improvement on the previous days and must have been a considerable morale boost for the RAF fighter pilots.

Sunday 21 July was a much quieter day and German bombers were committed against a convoy sailing west. However, for two German reconnaissance crews, this particular Sunday was memorable:

Oberleutnant **Friedrich Karl Runde, 4(F)/14**

On 21 July 1940, myself and [*Fw*] Willi Baden, my *Bordfunker*, took off from Villacoublay airfield near Paris. According to the weather forecast, we could expect clear skies and were ordered to fly a high altitude reconnaissance (at about 8,000m) and had some heavy photographic equipment installed in our plane. Before crossing the Channel, we landed at Cherbourg to refuel and then headed for the British Isles flying extremely low, between 10m and 50m, so as to avoid radar, and finally climbed to altitude only shortly before the British Coast. However, we found that there were clouds at 2,000m so we couldn't use our high-altitude photographic equipment so decided to undertake reconnaissance just using our eyes. However, it seemed useless and we returned to Cherbourg. We noticed just one enemy aircraft...

Flying Officer John Wray, No 1 Flying Training School

I was an instructor on the Advanced Training Squadron and on 21 July 1940, I was detailed to give an Instrument Flying Test to a pupil who, I think, was a Royal Marine [Lt Churchill]. For instrument flying, the pupil sat in the back cockpit of the Fairey Battle under what we called a Blind Flying Hood which covered the cockpit. This allowed the instructor to have a better all round view from the front where, apart from his instructional duties, he was also acting as a safety pilot avoiding collision or near misses with other aircraft.

We took off and headed towards Southampton, though I would be giving my pupil an instruction to turn 90° to avoid setting off the Southampton air raid sirens. I was allowing him to settle down before turning and we were at about 2,000ft. Suddenly, an Me 110 slid past us on the starboard side at about 100 to 200 yards. I had never seen an Me 110 up until this moment and had it not had a big black cross on the fuselage, I might have thought it was one of the many strange aircraft that flew out of Boscombe Down at that time.

He was overtaking us on a parallel course. I did a double take, not expecting to see German fighters so far west. In fact, the thought of encountering them at all was never in my mind so it is perhaps not surprising that I did nothing initially.

When he had got to about two o'clock to me, the rear gunner

opened fire and there was a loud bang on my Battle. Fortunately, there was a lot of fluffy cloud above me and so I slammed open the throttle, entered the cloud and headed north west on the supposition that his range would preclude him following me for long.

Having reached some degree of safety, my two priorities were firstly to escape and secondly to try and find out what damage had been done to my aircraft. The pupil was quite unaware of what was happening as he was under the hood. Communication was by Gosport Tube which, on the Battle, was obviously quite long and therefore required one to shout a bit. Informing him was low on my priorities though it did not occur to me at the time that he might have been what the bullet(s) hit!

Very soon, my first priority was overtaken by the second because my engine started to run very rough. Looking at the oil pressure gauge, I noticed the pressure dropping and the coolant gauge showed a rapid rise in temperature. It was clear that my engine was not going to keep going for much longer.

I decided to leave the cloud and hoped that the Me 110 had given up the chase. We came out just west of Warminster where I informed my pupil of what had occurred. My engine was now close to stopping altogether so it was clear that I would not make one of the five airfields that stretched north from Salisbury.

Although from the air Salisbury Plain looks fairly benign and flat, it does of course comprise large humps and hollows, shell holes and wooded areas, all a deterrent to a successful landing. When night flying, we on the Advanced Training Squadron had to teach landing on a dummy deck. This required a flare path comprising pillar lights and other equipment found on an aircraft carrier which gave quite a bright display on the airfield at night so against the threat of bombing, we transferred our night flying to a field at Shrewton on Salisbury Plain. It was in this field that I decided to attempt a landing.

I made my approach wheels down and then my engine stopped and it was clear that I wasn't going to make Shrewton so I raised the undercarriage and crash-landed on the side of a hill just short of

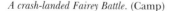
A crash-landed Fairey Battle. (Camp)

Shrewton. We skidded along and my port wing hit a grain silo. My head jerked forward and banged against the windscreen. I was not knocked out but was rather dazed.

The pupil, who was unhurt, came round and helped me out and sat me on a wing. He then ran to a nearby farmhouse where, after a few minutes, a woman appeared carrying a pot of tea. She and others looked after me until the ambulance and fire tender arrived about thirty minutes later. I was taken to Sick Quarters where I was examined by the Medical Officer. A few days later I was admitted to the RAF Hospital at Torquay.

The two German aircrew returned thinking nothing more of this incident but for them, the day was still not over:

Oberleutnant **Friedrich Karl Runde**

...At Cherbourg, the weather turned really fine and, after refuelling, we thought we would make another try despite having no orders telling us to do this. Coming back to the 'Other Side', the

Oblt Runde's Bf 110 after its repair...

...and repaint. (via Wray)

situation seemed not to have changed and as we didn't want to come back again without a result, we penetrated deeper. We then ran into a training aircraft and shot it down. Both of us felt very sad when we noticed the parachute of the young fellow didn't open.[3]

We turned back and then Willi Baden noticed fighters heading for us. I thought we would be able to escape into the clouds but these turned out to be some kind of summer fog which was dissipating with the sun rising higher. So that is how they got us. Both engines hit and despite managing to get away from them, I had to make a belly landing as both engines had seized.

[3] This was Acting Leading Airman J A Seed Royal Navy who, whilst flying solo in a Hawker Hart serial K6485 of No 1 Flying Training School, was sadly killed near Old Sarum airfield.

Pilot Officer Charles Davis, Red 2, 'A' Flight, 238 Squadron

Red Section was detailed to Raid X48 and took off at 1005 hrs, landed at 1035 hrs. I was Red 2 and we were ordered into line astern when enemy aircraft was seen at 6,000ft, ten miles south-east of base [Middle Wallop in Hampshire]. Enemy aircraft turned sharply east and Red Leader [Flt Lt Donald Turner] ordered Red 3 [Plt Off John Wigglesworth] and myself into cloud. I went other side of the cloud and got in a half attack when enemy aircraft came out. It was a running engagement with the enemy aircraft adopting most peculiar tactics. I fired short bursts whenever enemy aircraft came out of cloud. Finally it disappeared into a large cloud with smoke pouring from the starboard engine. Accuracy of aim was difficult owing to the bumpy conditions. Enemy aircraft did the most unusual manoeuvres – stall turns, half rolls etc.

Oblt Runde succeeded in crash-landing his Messerschmitt 110 so well that it was recovered by the RAF and by using parts from other captured Messerschmitt 110s, flew again. Curiously, John Wray inspected this aircraft later in the war not knowing until fifty-two years after the event that this aircraft was the one that had shot him down!

Nearly four hours later, the same three Hurricane pilots were in action again against another German aircraft from the same reconnaissance unit:

Leutnant Georg Thiel, 4(F)/14

4(F)/14 served as tactical reconnaissance under the VIth Army (von Kluge) during the Battle of France. From the beginning of July 1940, we were out at the disposal of V *Fliegerkorps* (*Generalleutnant* Robert Ritter von Griem).

On 21 July 1940, we started from the airport of Villacoublay, refuelled at Cherbourg and crossed the Channel at a height of between 5,500m and 6,500m. This was the absolute ceiling of our (worn out) Do 17.

After crossing the coast, I began filming as ordered. However, somewhere north of Southampton we got our first Spitfire [sic]/Hurricane salvo and dived down to hide in clouds. However, the oxygen system had been hit and the port engine had

The 'worn out Do 17 M' similar to that operated by 4(F)/14.

Georg Thiel's Do 17 in flames after the crash-landing. (via Cornwell)

Fw Bohnen about to be taken away to hospital. (via Cornwell)

stopped and was burning.

We lost height, tumbling down out of the clouds and then got hit again. *Uffz* Werner, the rear gunner, was clearly not able to ward off the RAF fighters with a single MG 15 machine gun. The pilot, *Fw* Bohnen, was unconscious for some time but anyhow we managed a crash landing and to get out of our 'bird' which was by then in flames.

It was two Sections of Hurricanes from 238 Squadron that had pounced on this unfortunate reconnaissance aircraft and shared its destruction:

Sergeant Leslie Batt, Yellow 3, 'A' Flight, 238 Squadron

First attack was carried out by Red Section [the same pilots that had shot down the Messerschmitt 110 from the same German unit earlier that day], line astern. Enemy then dived into cloud. I went south and under cloud and sighted enemy and attacked astern. Port engine was stopped and my fire concentrated on the starboard engine and enemy lost height rapidly. I broke away once and Red 1 attacked. I attacked again and stopped the starboard engine and then watched enemy crash-land without wheels. It then caught fire.

This quiet phase continued until 24 July. However, during the hours of darkness, the *Luftwaffe* was increasing its night missions, mainly mine laying in order to seal off ports and harbours in preparation for Operation *SEELOEWE*, the invasion of Great Britain. Such nocturnal forays were a nuisance for the embryonic RAF night fighter force. Nevertheless, on the night of 23/24 July 1940, Fg Off Glynn Ashfield of the Fighter Interception Unit with Plt Off Geoff Morris and Sgt Reg Leyland carried out the first ground radar assisted interception, claiming to have shot down a Dornier 17 into the Channel five miles south of Bognor Regis. The RAF would have to wait until 19 November 1940 for the first airborne radar assisted kill. The same night, another German bomber was lost but not to the guns of the RAF:

Hauptmann Volkmar Zenker, 2/KG 40

I was flying a Focke Wulf 200 *Condor* and we had started at Lueneburg in Germany on 23 July 1940. We refuelled at Brest and there we were loaded with two tons of magnetic mines. Our orders were to drop these in the shipping lanes at Belfast Harbour. We only managed to drop three mines before disaster struck.

An FW 200 of I/KG 40. (Wachtel)

I had descended from 1,800m over the Irish Sea. The engines were idling as I was hoping not to be detected. During the first part of the mission, I was flying at 100m but then I opened the throttles very

A Condor of I/KG 40 over the Irish Sea – the low altitude left little room for error. (Hintze)

slowly hoping to lose more height and to get rid of the last mine which was stuck in its holder. I succeeded but by now we were at 15m altitude. When I opened the throttles further, the two port engines stopped and the plane banked suddenly. In order to avoid the wingtip hitting the water, I stopped the starboard engines and ditched. The plane had not run out of fuel, by the way, but there had been an air blockage in the fuel lines caused by the long glide with idled engines.

After the ditching, the plane sank pretty fast. The *Bordfunker* [*Uffz* Heinz Hoecker] and *Bordschuetz* [*Gefr* Leo Hohmann] were able to leave by the main door and got out the dinghy...

Unteroffizier Heinz Hoecker, 2/KG 40

Because of the impact, the plane was full of water very quickly. In the cockpit I saw my comrades in the water looking for an exit. As a result of this, I swam to the exit at the back, called my comrade Hohmann and told him to get the dinghy ready. I pushed open the door and got out. In the pitch dark, I called to the others. All that I had in the dinghy was a distress signal in a tin and the dinghy was not fully inflated...

Hauptmann **Volkmar Zenker**

...My co-pilot [*Fw* Willi Andreas], *Bordmechaniker* [*Uffz* Rudolf Wagner] and myself were caught in the cockpit because the escape door jammed. I tried to send them aft but we were already under water. I dived through the aircraft and managed to get to where the water had risen close to the door. I waited for the other two for a moment and then joined the two who were swimming with the inflated dinghy. We expected the missing crew members, who were uninjured and able to swim, to join us but I think that they had panicked and had tried to leave by the hatch at the top of the cockpit or through windows which were too small. Because we did not know how long the Condor would float, we did not dare go back in. In any case, after a few minutes it sank.

The dinghy proved to be our next problem. The self-inflating mechanism did not work and the CO_2 bottle was empty. We had to pump the dinghy up by using bellows which took us nearly three quarters of an hour. One oar was lost during the hubbub so we could not reach the coast under cover of darkness although we tried hard, knowing that we were not too far from the Southern Ireland border...

Unteroffizier **Heinz Hoecker**

...In the morning, we noticed a ship on the horizon which was heading towards us. I realised that *Hptm* Zenker had exhausted himself and so I took command. In case of capture, I reminded them that we had been told that we should say we had been on a reconnaissance flight with a Do 17. Then I searched *Hptm* Zenker's pockets and threw overboard everything that could be useful to the British. The ship came towards us – the crew stood on deck with rifles loaded; the officer had a pistol. We were ordered "Hands up!" – I had already fired off two signal flares and thrown the pistol and the rest of the flares overboard. One at a time we climbed up the ladder and after we had been searched, the sailors gave us some rum – I was grateful for that because by then, I had had enough.

On our way into Belfast, I saw a ship at the bottom of the harbour. When I asked how it had sunk, I was told it had caught fire[4]...

The Germans, when interrogated, stuck to their story as proved by the diary entry for Flag Officer Belfast:

On the morning of 24 July, three German airmen were rescued from

---

[4] The SS *Troutpool* had sunk on 20 July, the victim of a magnetic mine dropped by the *Luftwaffe* the night before.

a rubber float by the anti-submarine trawler HMS *Paynter* close to Blackhead and were landed at Larne. When interrogated, they stated that their machine, an He 111, had crashed in the early hours of the morning during a reconnaissance flight over the area with the loss of two lives.

For the remainder of the month, the pattern was the same – attacks on convoys and coastal targets, interspersed with fighter sweeps, both of which were keenly opposed by the RAF. At this time, the much feared *Stuka* was still making its presence felt, albeit on a smaller scale than in the Battle of France:

Oberleutnant Klaus Ostmann, 8/StG 1

I was posted to StG1 in Bretagne in July 1940. Coming from Koeln, I flew over the first traces of the battles in France. Having seen the destruction, I can understand what our *Stukas* could achieve and had to achieve. I phoned my new *Geschwader* from the airfield at Compiègne and asked them to pick me up. The phone line was excellent – a direct line from Compiègne to the Channel coast! Later that day, a liaison aircraft took me to StG1 – on our way, we circled over destroyed traffic junctions, bridges and buildings.

The *Geschwader* had its HQ in a château near Caen. There I reported to the *Kommodore*, *Maj* Walter Hagen – the first holder of the *Ritterkreuz* I have ever faced. I am posted to 8/StG1 – the *Gruppen Kommandeur* was *Hptm* Helmut Mahlke, my *Staffelkapitaen* was *Oblt* Guenter Skambraks. We were billeted in a villa in Falaise – in our opinion a little bit dilapidated. The airfield is only a narrow strip, completely surrounded by bushes – well camouflaged but aeronautically very difficult. I am assigned Ju 87 'Gustav' – J9+GK.

For missions, we moved to the forward airfield of Theville near Cherbourg. My first mission was from there on 25 July. The *Gruppe* crossed the Channel, climbing to 4,500m.

Oblt *Klaus Ostmann – the nautical flavour of the badge is because III/StG 1 was originally designated I(Stuka)/186 and destined to operate from an aircraft carrier.* (Ostmann)

Below us the shimmering sea. It was difficult to estimate your own height and very often you thought that you would plunge into the water when you pointed the aircraft's nose down. Then in the distance a dark line appears – the English coast. Flying over the water had strained our nerves and this feeling was now intensifying.

Stukas of Stab/StG1 *over the Channel.* (Grahl)

Very often we were able to listen to the enemy's radio traffic which tells us that their fighters have already taken off. Well, we saw them high above us before we attacked. They looked like birds of prey waiting to pounce. It was an uneasy feeling. For good reasons, our own radio traffic had been kept to essentials. Our target was a convoy near Portland Bill. I had not seen anything – it is difficult to spot a ship at sea level – but the formation had already started to dive. After all the tension, a feeling of relief comes over you. You are determined to get the target and there was only one aim – to hit the target. One does not notice the *Flak* which shoots by and bursts either side. Now I have picked the target, dropped the bombs and by taking wild evasive action, I follow the formation which is already joining up again. But now our machine guns are hammering and I can see the eight trails of a Spitfire's tracer bullets trying to reach me again and again, like ghostly fingers. A few times, you can hear a crack but the plane's fuselage is wide and if nothing vital has been hit, the faithful *Stuka* can take a lot of hits like that. I have succeeded in shaking off the last attacker and without any problems, I landed on the advanced airfield. All of us have come under heavy fire. The *Staffelkapitaen's* aircraft has received a hit in the oil tank and only with great difficulty could he find his way home. Everything was smeared with oil and so he had to make an emergency landing at a small airfield near Cherbourg. I led the formation back.

However, for the last six days of July 1940 the weather yet again continued to play its part in limiting German air operations. Of interest were the attacks undertaken by the specialised fighter-bomber unit

Erprobungsgruppe 210. This unit had flown its first mission on 13 July 1940 and during the weeks that followed, had flown a number of missions for the loss of just two Messerschmitt 110s and their crews. One pilot kept a diary of his time with the unit only for it to fall into the RAF's hands when he was shot down and killed on 15 August 1940. Still in existence today in the RAF's Air Historical Branch, the diary entry for 29 July 1940 gives a clear idea of what it was like flying fighter-bomber missions against convoys and how the writer almost became the unit's third combat loss of the war:

Leutnant Erich Beudel, 1/*ErprGr* 210

My second war flight. A Dornier 17 has reported an English convoy of sixty ships sailing northwards from the Thames Estuary. *ErprGr* 210 takes off from St Omer at 1635 hrs; eight Bf 110 bombers of 2 *Staffel* and three Bf 110 C-6s of 1 *Staffel* fly over Dunkirk and meet thirty Bf 110 C-2s of ZG 26 who are acting as fighter escort on account of probable clear skies. Thirty minutes flying northwards at sea level, then ten minutes climbing towards the clouds at 4,500ft. The bombers attack at 1715 hrs just off Orfordness… At the same time two Hurricane squadrons approach from the left, one below us and one above. The Chief makes a tight climbing turn and I fall back a bit, then it is a flat out climb. I have to abandon the idea of getting on the tail of one of the lower Englishmen because the upper formation comes at me from above and the right. Straightening up for a moment, I fire a short burst at a singleton who comes past me but he doesn't fall. The next moment my gunner shouts something unintelligible and a hail of fire rips through my whole aircraft from the right. The intercom packs up completely but in another two seconds, I am in the clouds. I circle to take stock and decide to beat it. Above the clouds I come across three Bf 110s, the Chief and two aircraft of ZG 26 who want to attack again. I feel inclined to join them but my gunner calls out "I am wounded; let's go home!" So I head for the Dutch Coast. My trim tabs are shot away and oil spurts from the starboard engine. At last at 1805 hrs I land at St Omer with tyres shot through. My aircraft has suffered about thirty hits; one shot struck an ammunition drum and exploded all the cartridges. Other hits in engines, cockpit, wings and landing flaps. Result of the attack – one hit on a 1,000 ton ship and one hit on an 8,000 ton ship. ZG 26 bagged four Hurricanes without loss.[5]

Very little changed for the last two days of the month and it appeared that the RAF had survived the first month of the Battle of Britain even

[5] The attack was against Convoy CAT which was defended by just one RAF squadron. 151 Squadron attacked in two separate flights (hence Beudel thought two squadrons) and suffered just two Hurricanes damaged.

though, as yet, it had not received the undivided and unwelcome attention of the *Luftwaffe*. For the *Luftwaffe*, its bombers had little chance so far to attack en masse, targets being more suitable to attacks by smaller formations or by *Stukas*, easily defended by its fighters. Nevertheless, German bomber and reconnaissance aircraft had roamed the length and breadth of the United Kingdom and its surrounding waters, normally with impunity, and at the same time had found that there was no sign of any major weakness in the RAF's defences either by day or, it now seemed, by night. However, August 1940 would see changes to the German battle plan and the RAF fighter pilots being severely tested.

2
The Pace Quickens – August 1940

From the viewpoint of German bomber crews, the first seven days of August 1940 were, because of poor weather conditions, an anti-climax. What effort was expended was done so against convoys or harbours but of note was an attack against the Boulton Paul Aircraft Factory at Norwich on the afternoon of 1 August. Four 250 kilogram bombs slightly damaged the factory and nearby railway yard, setting fire to a timber yard and injuring in excess of forty civilians. Despite the close proximity of the fighter airfield at Coltishall, the attacker got away unscathed.

Mine laying and attacks on harbour installations took place that night and on the nights that followed. Of particular interest was that the *Luftwaffe* reported dropping 300 kilograms of leaflets in and around London detailing the *Fuehrer*'s latest speech on the night of 2/3 August – other major cities received similar deliveries on subsequent nights. Also, despite the weather, German reconnaissance aircraft were very active and in addition to maritime targets were also making particular notes of airfields and the RAF aircraft observed there – perhaps the *Luftwaffe* was considering a change in target? By the middle of the month, it would be clear as to what the *Luftwaffe*'s targets were.

8 August would see a dramatic change in the level of air activity. At 1930 hrs on 7 August, German sources had reported a large convoy of an unknown number of ships 10 kilometres south of Dungeness headed west. Early the next morning, this convoy, now totalling in the region of eighteen ships, was reported south east of the Isle of Wight. Convoy CW9, code named PEEWIT, was about to receive the undivided attention of the *Luftwaffe*'s bombers.

Oberleutnant Klaus Ostmann, 8/StG 1

Another flight to the forward airfield was not in vain. There we were, standing by, lying on our deck chairs. On the radio, you could hear the popular hit song *Auf dem Dach Welt* [On Top of the World]. Even today I can still hear this catchy tune. Suddenly there was the order *Grosseinsatz* – big attack. We were briefed to attack a well protected convoy 10 miles south-west of the Isle of Wight which had been attacked by E-boats at night. Take off time from Theville was 0930 hrs.

Again, the long flight over the water was quite nerve-racking but the complete *Geschwader* was in action and the sky was full of *Stukas*. This gave you a reassuring feeling. This time I saw more than I did on my first mission – the smoke trails were the characteristic mark of our target, the convoy. We are the last *Staffel* and so our job was the hardest. We would be longer in the range of fire, we would be the last to fly back and a tempting target for the enemy fighters – the Devil takes the hindmost!

Now we are over the target. Down we go from a high altitude. I had to correct the bomb run the whole time because the ships are spreading out – zigzagging wildly.

I think I stayed over the target too long and was separated from the rest of the *Staffel*. Flying wild evasive manoeuvres, I tried to catch up with the formation. There was a big cumulus cloud ahead. I flew into the cloud and think myself safe but hardly have I left it than enemy fighters attacked from above. They knew that something had to come out of this cloud and so they were able to pick me off. There was a loud bang in my plane. An indescribable blow hit my right arm and knee. The aircraft nose dived but then I regained consciousness. Using my left arm, I pulled the plane out of the dive just above sea level. Spasmodically, a stream of blood came out of my knee. As good as I can, I applied a tourniquet to my right leg with the laces of my map board. Now *Oblt* Karl Lion, *Ia* of III/StG 1 was flying next to me and encouraged me to hold on. The way back takes about fifty minutes – an eternity. I was really in a bad way. As soon as I see the French coast, all my energies came back. At full speed I approached the airfield. I brought the plane down, it bounced a few times and then skidded to the left – the undercarriage had also been hit. Then I lost consciousness – when I came to, I was on my way to a field hospital at Valognes near Cherbourg. I did not return to StG 1 until August 1941.

The sole RAF squadron to intercept this attack was the Hurricane-equipped 145 Squadron. Claiming two destroyed, nine probably destroyed and five damaged, to tie down who for certain damaged *Oblt* Ostmann's *Stuka* is difficult but the following RAF pilot could be considered as the likely protagonist:

Oblt Klaus Ostmann returns to the front, exactly a year after being wounded.
(Ostmann)

Squadron Leader John Peel, 'A' Flight, 145 Squadron

...I attacked another Ju 87 some distance behind with a beam attack but guns stopped after a two second burst. Enemy aircraft dropped to sea level and flew off in a right-hand turn, unsteady and probably badly damaged.

Stukas of I/StG 1 off the English south coast. (Grahl)

Heavily escorted, the attack was not in fact carried out by all of StG 1 but twenty-nine *Stukas* of I/StG 3 together with twenty-eight from III/StG 1. After losing just one *Stuka* from III/StG 1, it was the turn of forty-nine *Stukas* from I and III/StG 2 to attack the convoy again just after lunch time – this time no *Stukas* were lost. Still, the convoy sailed on so it was attacked a third time by twenty-two *Stukas* from *Hptm* Paul Werner Hozzel's I/StG 1 and an undisclosed number of *Stukas* from *Hptm* Walter Sigel's I/StG 3 and *Hptm* Waldemar Plewig's II/StG 77. It was hoped that this time, the *Stukas* would annihilate the convoy:

Hauptmann **Waldemar Plewig,** *Gruppen Kommandeur* **II/StG 77**

In the area around Caen, several *Geschwader* were ready for action on 8 August 1940. The results of reconnaissance flights reported a very large convoy near the Isle of Wight but because of apparent bad weather, the *Oberbefehlshaber der Luftwaffe* did not give the okay for action. With the permission of the *Geschwader* I went up in my *Gruppe's* Do 17 to make my own reconnaissance and found that an attack against clearly recognisable shipping targets was certainly possible. So, after midday, we finally received clearance for three *Gruppen* of *Stukas* to go into action. Besides the *Gruppen* commanded by *Hptms* Hozzel and Sigel, my *Gruppe* was to assemble at 1600 hrs over Cherbourg and to carry out a large scale attack.

My *Gruppe* started as ordered but noticed that one of the other *Gruppen* was not ready for take off. Climbing steadily, we proceeded to the gathering point. As we approached the coast, I realised that the third *Gruppe* was already hanging over the Channel above us, long before the stated time. Our own fighters must have split up as only a few Bf 109s and Bf 110s were to be seen. The majority of the fighter escort must have flown to the target area with the *Gruppe* of early starters. Only this could explain why my *Gruppe*, when approaching the convoy, flew right into the arms of the RAF fighters which had been lured up by the first *Gruppe*; our escort then split up, the first *Gruppe* already returning with the escort whilst my far weaker escort had to fight against overwhelming odds.

Under the circumstances, there was no turning back and I ordered the three *Staffeln* to attack. I, with the reinforced *Stabs Kette*, waited until the end. As we could see more and more

Hptm *Waldemar Plewig – he was awarded the* Ritterkreuz *whilst in captivity.* (Plewig)

enemy fighters appearing above us, I decided not to climb up to the usual altitude and started the attack from about 4,000m. After the three *Staffeln* had attacked their targets, I chose mine and went into a dive and released my bombs from about 600m. The Spitfires and Hurricanes dived with us but we were able to observe some near misses. It did not matter so much about direct hits as our bombs were fitted with delayed fuses so that they didn't explode on impact but after penetrating the water, thus causing a strong pressure wave.

Now I attempted to throw off my adversaries by irregular flying at sea level – we always flew off that way as it gave fighters less of a chance to hit us. However, during the descent, I was repeatedly shot at. My gunner, *Fw* Schauer, fired until he was hit, presumably in the neck and thigh as I noticed a jet of blood. In the meantime, I was hit in the right arm and right calf and had to fly with my left hand. At the same time, the oxygen supply was hit as was a box of ammunition by tracer bullets. When the plane started to show signs of burning on the right side, I decided to bale out. My gunner did not reply over the intercom and I could see him hanging lifelessly in the harness. As he did not react to my order to throw off the canopy and I had levelled off above the water and the plane was well alight, I decided to jump at the last moment. I had failed in my efforts to throw out the gunner – he was certainly dead and I hoped that his body might be washed up somewhere. So, I said goodbye to my companion and friend Schauer.

I must have been low when I jumped and got caught up in the lines. Although it was summer, the sea was rough and I had great difficulty in freeing myself from the harness, being constantly pushed under by the water. My knife was strapped to my right leg and I had to get it with my left hand. When I finally cut myself free of the lines, my parachute was still inflated and I did not know which way I was drifting – either towards France, England or the Atlantic. I managed to get rid of the parachute. Still, I might be lucky and washed up against one of the 'Udet' lifeboats.

The kapok life jacket favoured by Hptm *Plewig and other bomber crews, here worn by* Fw Robert Ciuraj *and* Lt Bernhard Sartor *of 4/KG 51.* (Ciuraj)

For the moment, I was glad that I was wearing a kapok lifejacket which originated from the Merchant Navy and was fitted with a 'Stuart' collar which kept my head well out of the water. It is difficult to describe what happened after. I can only say that during the minutes and hours that I drifted in the water, all my past life passed before me like a kaleidoscope. However, I certainly had the will to live.

When it got dark, I noticed a small ship pass me. My yellow marker dye was still working but who could see this in the heavy swell? Again and again, British and German fighters flew over me and I tried to make myself seen. After four or five hours, a corvette passed close to me. She disappeared but came back and I saw that they were lowering a small boat and I think that two sailors were trying to reach me. After many attempts, they succeeded and threw me a rope which I gripped with my left hand and they heaved me into the boat. Now started a far more difficult phase, namely to get the boat back to the corvette. Several attempts were made and finally they succeeded and a rope was lowered which they thought I could grip. One of the sailors had to tie me to the rope and I was heaved onto the deck. There I had a great reception – to this day, I remember they wanted to feed me on rum and white bread. However, all the sea water I had swallowed had filled me up and when I asked for a bowl, they offered me more rum – I couldn't speak enough English! Anyway, I was very sick and I then felt better and was taken below.

I was admitted to a naval hospital in Portsmouth in the late evening. Here too I was well treated. One of the nurses found a Walther PPK in the back pocket of my trousers – she kept it and asked me not to say anything about it as she wanted it as a souvenir. Later a military chaplain came to see me and then I remember waking up in a small ward surrounded by doctors and nurses. The surgeon was very worried about me – he reminded me of my uncle who was also a doctor. Unfortunately, I was later transferred to a hospital at Woolwich but I shall never forget the Naval Hospital, most of all the people there.

The aim by the *Luftwaffe* to annihilate the convoy almost succeeded – only four ships arrived unscathed at Swanage later that evening, the *Stukas* having sunk seven and damaged another thirteen. The air battle over the convoy had been particularly fierce which enabled the *Stukas* to achieve their success. Despite the RAF claiming to have shot down thirty-three German aircraft, the *Luftwaffe* lost eight *Stukas* with a further seven damaged – the human cost was thirteen aircrew killed, three prisoners of war and seven wounded. Three executive officers were lost – in addition to the *Gruppen Kommandeur* of II/StG 77, *Hptm* Horst-Hennig Schmack, the *Staffel Kapitaen* of 4/StG 77 was killed and *Oblt* Martin Mueller, *Adjutant* of I/StG 3 was taken prisoner. A further nine fighters and seven fighter aircrew were killed. For the RAF, it had been a hard battle – despite the Germans claiming to have shot down forty-seven fighters, only fourteen RAF fighters were lost but, more crucially, twelve pilots were killed.

For the RAF, this had been an ominous start to the month's fighting. The next two days were quiet – in the words of the writer of the *Luftwaffe Fuehrungsstab* diary: "nothing of particular importance to report." Sporadic attacks were carried out against various minor targets and then, on 11 August, it was the turn of the Junkers 88 to enter the battle en masse.

This time, the target was the harbour and associated installations at Portland. Thirty-eight Junkers 88s from I and II/KG 54 (with two Heinkel 111s as air sea rescue support – obviously a lesson learnt from the 8 August battles) took off at 0935 hrs and reported hits on the oil pipeline, mole, floating dock, loading bridges and railway lines. A fuel storage tank was set on fire and at least two freighters and a destroyer damaged as well as a small ship being sunk in Weymouth harbour. Again, the German fighter escort was massive, forcing the RAF to commit eight fighter squadrons. The German tactics succeeded in drawing many of the RAF fighters away, thus allowing the bombers to reach their target but it did not prevent the loss of four bombers, including that flown by the *Gruppen Kommandeur* of II/KG 54, *Maj* Kurt Leonhardy. Meanwhile, the last actions of this phase of the Battle of Britain were being fought further to the east with attacks against shipping and convoys by a number of *Kampfgeschwadern* and *Erprobungsgruppe* 210.

Overnight, Heinkel 111s of a number of units were in action against harbours, aircraft factories and shipping. A rare nocturnal success was when the *Gruppen Kommandeur* of II/KG 27's Heinkel 111 was hit by anti-aircraft fire and crashed in Dorset – *Maj* Friedrich-Karl Schlichting and his crew, which also included *Maj* Hans-Juergen Brehmer, were all captured. However, it soon became clear as 12 August 1940 progressed that airfields and radar stations were now on the target list.

The first objectives for the day were the radar stations at Dover, Dunkirk, Pevensey and Rye – heavily escorted, *Erprobungsgruppe* 210 succeeded in putting three sites temporarily out of action for no loss to themselves. Shortly afterwards, attacks were carried out by II/KG 2 and another Dornier 17 unit against the airfields of Lympne and Hawkinge with the sole aim of preventing these airfields being used as a fighter base. Lympne was, according to the *Luftwaffe* crews involved, heavily bombed but this did not affect the operational effectiveness of the airfield. Hawkinge, attacked later during the day as well, was operational again within twenty-four hours.

The next major raid appeared on the radar screens further west just before lunchtime. Sixty-three Junkers 88s from all three *Gruppe* of KG 51 lifted off from the airfields of Melun, Orly and Etampes–Montdesir at about 1130 hrs Central European Time. Their targets were Portsmouth Harbour and the radar station at Ventnor on the Isle of Wight. Again, the escort was massive, made up from three different Messerschmitt 110 *Geschwader* and three Messerschmitt 109 *Geschwader*. The RAF response was to throw eight fighter squadrons at the approaching armada and what followed was memorable for many of the German crews involved:

Oberleutnant **Werner Luederitz, *Stab*/KG 51**

The aircraft of the *Geschwader Stab* were stationed at Orly near Paris, along with II/KG 51. On 11 August 1940, the weather forecast (obtained from the special meteorological units and KG 40) was for good weather for an attack against the British Isles the following day, mainly because of high pressure over the Azores.

On the morning of 12 August, the *Kommodore*, *Oberst Dr* Hans Fisser, received by telephone from the Chief of *Luftflotte* 3 in Paris, *Generalfeldmarschall* Hugo Sperrle, the order to carry out an attack by all serviceable aircraft against the radar station at Ventnor (south-east Isle of Wight) and the harbour at Portsmouth. The aim was to knock out the radar station and to destroy the harbour facilities, yards, fuel dumps and ships at Portsmouth. The secondary objective was to lure out the British fighters which would be destroyed by our escorting fighters allowing us to establish air superiority over southern England.

Werner Luederitz (seen here as a Leutnant*).* (Luederitz)

The *Kommodore* decided that the *Geschwader Kette* would take part in the attack on the radar station. The bomb load for the attack was either two SC 1,000 kilogram bombs or four 250 kilogram bombs – my aircraft coded 9K+AA was loaded with two 1,000 kilogram bombs.[1]

We rendezvoused over Le Havre at 5,000m altitude and headed for England. After overflying the western half of the Isle of Wight, we turned eastward and split up – *Geschwader Kette* and II *Gruppe* towards Ventnor from the north, whilst I and III *Gruppen* turned towards Portsmouth. We came down at a 70° angle in a loose formation from 4,000m, released the bombs at 1,200m and intended to climb from 800m to transit level and fly home. However, the port engine quickly lost power and stopped – during our dive, we had taken a lot of *Flak* and shrapnel had hit the port engine and interrupted the fuel supply. We remained far behind the formation which was climbing and I took

---

[1] The total number of bombs to be dropped by KG 51 were briefed as eight SC 1,000, thirty-six SC 500 and thirty-six SC 250 (SC were thin cased high explosive bombs) in addition to six PC 500 bombs (PC bombs were armour-piercing and used against warships) and four Flam 250 bombs (flammable oil bombs).

the necessary steps for asymmetric flight (feathering the propeller, trimming and dumping all unnecessary fuel and equipment, except for parachutes and machine guns). We found ourselves alone over the Isle of Wight at about 1,000m flying south and still trying to gain height. There was no sign of our escort – they were in dogfights further north.

Ventnor and its radar station above it as seen by a German aircraft in 1943. (Wenger)

Generalfeldmarschall *Hugo Sperrle*. (Wittmann)

The cockpit armament of a KG 51 Ju 88. (Ciuraj)

Shortly after crossing the coast, we were attacked by three Hurricanes [sic], one after another and all from behind. We could see the bullets hitting our control surfaces – a few shots even went through the cockpit without doing any great damage. However, our impaired flying performance was further affected by damage to the flying controls. The Hurricanes were, of course, much faster and on each attack let off a short burst. 9K+AA was fitted with side machine guns in the cockpit so that we were able to fire at the departing fighters which exposed their undersides. I do not know if we had any success. As a result of evasive manoeuvres, we had lost height very quickly and were, after five or six attacks, about 50m above sea level and expected to ditch. However, as we had been told that coastal waters around the United Kingdom had been mined in expectation of an invasion, we turned towards land. After further attacks whilst we were very low, I put the aircraft down wheels up. We crashed through hedges and the aircraft burst into flames...

Claims for Junkers 88s by the RAF were many and confused. However, it is likely that Spitfires of 152 Squadron intercepted the Ventnor attackers and one combat report does seem to match with *Oblt* Luederitz's account of the battle:

Sergeant Edmund Shepperd, White 2, 152 Squadron

I was on patrol at 15,000ft when I met a formation of about twelve Junkers 88s. 'A' Flight formed into line astern and did a dive attack onto the formation which split up. I did an astern attack on one Ju 88 with a burst of eight seconds and Plt Off Bayles confirms that the port engine burst into flames... I then attacked another Ju 88 at 4,000ft with full deflection, closing to 100 yards with a burst of four seconds. I did a second attack with a range of 200 yards and finished my ammunition. I followed the aircraft down until it force-landed in a field and burst into flames.

Oberleutnant Werner Luederitz

...Surrounded by flames, I felt that the plane had stopped. I undid my harness, fell out the port side and clawed my way out of the sea of flames. My clothes, parachute and life jacket were burning so I rolled in the grass. I saw the other two crew members – Franz Schad and Adam Nothelfer who had escaped to starboard. Schad had also extinguished his burning clothes but Nothelfer, still in a state of shock, was sitting on the grass, his parachute still burning. I shouted at him to roll in the grass but there was no reaction but Schad, who was nearby, knocked him over and put the flames out. Nothing was to be seen of the *Kommodore*. We moved about 50m away from the burning aircraft and were surrounded by civilians wearing armbands and carrying rifles and a few unarmed men in uniform and members of

Oberst Dr *Hans Fisser (right), Kommodore of KG 51, killed in action 12 August 1940; the pilot being awarded the Iron Cross, Oblt Eberhard Wildermuth of 8/KG 51, was also shot down on 12 August 1940.* (Wildermuth)

the public. The aircraft was by now enveloped in flames and we could hear the remaining ammunition exploding.

Schad and myself had second and third degree burns on our faces, hands and throat whilst Nothelfer was also burnt on his back and legs. A little grey haired lady first quietened a hysterical young Army officer who was shouting at us (he wore a beret with a red pom-pom) then tried to dress our wounds. We were taken by ambulance to a small hospital and then, because of the severity of our burns, to a large military hospital near Cowes [Osborne House].

The attack on Ventnor was a success but the radar station was back on line by 15 August 1940. In addition to the loss of the *Geschwader Kommodore* and his crew, *Oblt* Hans-Joachim Flegel and his crew from 6/KG 51 were shot down into the sea off the Isle of Wight. However, as one air battle was taking place over the Isle of Wight, another more bloody battle was taking place over Portsmouth Harbour:

Unteroffizier **Karl Zimmermann, 3/KG 51**

We were based at Melun – 12 August was a nice sunny day but we were destined not to enjoy it. We got into our aircraft, started our engines and warmed them up for a short while. One 3 *Staffel* aircraft after another took off with a heavy bomb load intended for Portsmouth. Flying between 4,000m and 5,000m, it was quiet – no ship or fighter aircraft were seen. When we got closer to the Isle of Wight, *Flak* bursts appeared below us. However, the closer we got to the target, more and more RAF fighters were seen. Around us – above, below and next to us, things were in turmoil. We had almost arrived at the target when – oh my goodness! – a Spitfire was behind us and there was a bang and the instrument panel was shattered. I have trouble with the controls, the port engine seizes up and the crew is screaming. The *Bordfunker* [*Ogefr* Oskar Hansmann] bleeds from his hand, the *Beobachter* [*Gefr* Theo Dickel] has been hit seriously whilst I have a bullet and some splinters in my left leg. Only the *Bordmechaniker* [*Ogefr* Karl-Heinz Fahrenheim] in the gondola had not been hit. I then lost control of the aircraft and shouted "Get out! Bale out!" The *Bordfunker* threw off the canopy roof and with great difficulty, we struggled out of the plane. Wriggling, we all hang on our parachutes – we could hear bullets hissing past us and saw other planes going down in flames. I landed in a vegetable patch at Haslar, spraining my legs. Hardly had I touched the ground when four men came up to me armed with rifles and pistols. I was frisked and taken to a car. Afterwards, I had lunch, was interrogated and then taken to a hospital at Netley. By the way, my comrade Dickel lost his life.

Uffz Karl Zimmermann's capture was related in the 13 August 1940 edition of the local newspaper, their account appearing far more dramatic than the German pilot remembers:

> …One of the crew of a German aeroplane who landed by parachute during an air raid in Southern England yesterday was held up with a gun by a farm groom and afterwards handed over to the police and military authorities.
>
> The German, who was wounded in the left leg and was given first aid treatment, was seen by a doctor on arrival at a local police station and was given a meal and made comfortable. It is understood that another of the occupants of the plane landed in the sea and was drowned.
>
> The injured aviator who is between 25 and 35 years of age was dressed in a grey zip-fastener flying suit. He landed by parachute in a farm garden only a few yards away from where the groom, William Reid, was standing. Seizing a double-barrelled gun, Mr Reid rushed to the spot and at the same time Mr W S Jeffreys, who had been in his mother's house nearby and saw the airman descending, arrived at the scene carrying a revolver.
>
> The wounded German was covered by Mr Reid whilst Mr Jeffreys, with assistance, searched him. First aid was rendered by Mr Jeffreys who took the German to his house and gave him brandy…

Meanwhile, over the Harbour itself, the destruction of another Junkers 88 was witnessed by many onlookers, one of whom recorded the attack in great detail:

Alexander McKee

> …a Junkers plunged headlong, twisting and jerking…like a dead thing it dropped out of sight like a falling leaf… The Ju 88 which we saw come down had its tail blown off by the gunners of the *Courbet* [a French battleship which was serving as a depot ship for the Free French Navy] which explains the falling leaf act…

Three out of the four crew from this aircraft were lucky to survive such a traumatic shooting down:

Oberleutnant Eberhard Wildermuth, 8/KG 51

> In the morning of 12 August 1940, III/KG 51, then stationed at Etampes–Montdesir, received orders to attack shipping in Portsmouth Harbour. With my *Kette* (*Oblt* Wilhelm Noelken in 9K+AS and *Uffz* Richard Metschuldt in 9K+ES) I was also to provide cover to the rest

Oblt *Eberhard Wildermuth, June 1940.*
(Wildermuth)

of the *Gruppe* against enemy fighters. At the time the order was given, some technical modifications were being carried out on my plane and I was therefore unable to start immediately. However, I succeeded to fly after the others and catch them up over the Channel. There was not a cloud in the sky when at midday, we approached Portsmouth across the Isle of Wight. Over the Isle of Wight, there was a thick layer of smoke caused by the *Flak* – incredibly, we flew at an altitude of 4,000m right through a witch's cauldron of exploding shells.

The view from the cockpit of a 8/KG 51 Ju 88 during a practice dive attack, August 1940. (Wildermuth)

We had orders to dive down on targets in the harbour and not to level out higher than 1,200m, which meant that we had to dive in between the barrage balloons at 2,000m, keep the target in our sights and at 1,200m press the button which pulled us out of the dive and released the bombs at the same time. The plane then carried on falling to about 700m – during the dive, the plane was under heavy attack from the *Flak* and shaken by the explosions all around.

I had dropped the bombs and pulled back the plane to about 1,500m when suddenly, I lost all feeling in the stick – the controls had gone and the plane went into a dreaded spin. Through the throat microphone I yelled "I can't hold the plane – get out!" and threw off the cockpit roof and unclipped my seat belt. The *Beobachter* sitting alongside me [*Oblt* Otto Staerk] did the same. The centrifugal forces created by the spin pressed me into the perspex dome of the front of the cockpit – the force was so strong that I was unable to move my arms. From where I was, I could see the altimeter – 1,400m, 1,300m,

1,200m… I looked at the *Beobachter* who was pressed into the cockpit next to me and I was sure that now the 'stove had gone out'.

Then, suddenly, a rush of air dragged both of us out. After the roar of the engines racing at super speed, everything went deathly quiet. I saw the left wing whizzing past my head and shortly afterwards, heard the air hissing into my parachute. I had released the parachute quite automatically and was now gradually floating towards the waters of the harbour. Looking up, I noticed that my *Beobachter*, dangling above me on his parachute, was taking photos of me – he was a real photo fan and never went on a flight without his camera dangling around his neck. I waved to him and wondered if I would be able to swim to the French coast! With interest, I watched tracer bullets being fired from the ground and ten seconds later, I splashed into the water and was engulfed by my parachute.

Luckily, the water was not deep so I was able to get a breath of air now and then if I stood on tiptoe. At last, I managed to get out of the straps and in the meantime, my *Beobachter* had also freed himself from his parachute and, 50m away, I saw my *Bordfunker* [*Uffz* Droese] who had also parachuted down. Of the *Bordmechaniker* [*Uffz* Roesch] there was no sign.

For another half an hour, we stayed in the water whilst the planes who followed us dropped their bombs. Some of them exploded right next to us and sent up fountains of water all around us. Finally, the raid finished and a group of perhaps ten British soldiers who had previously manned the *Flak* guns fished us out of the water and brought us ashore.

I remember taking off my soaking wet flying suit and putting it in the sun to dry. I never saw it again – presumably a soldier took it as a souvenir. One of them seeing my unhappy face said "You're lucky – for you the war is over" – all I could say was "S**t!"

We were then taken to a nearby Naval Officers' Mess and were given something to eat. By now, I was so tired (we had spent the previous night sightseeing in Paris and had not returned to Etampes until early in the morning!). Then, after taking off my wet

Oblt Wildermuth *and* Uffz Droese; *behind them is* Ju 88 A-1, *Werk Nummer 4078 coded 9K+BS which crashed into Portsmouth Harbour on 12 August 1940.* (Wildermuth)

French sailors from the battleship Courbet *after having recovered items from the crashed Ju 88 which, sadly, include tatters of uniform belonging to* Uffz Roesch. (via Saunders)

clothes, I lay down on a bed and slept like the dead…

Portsmouth had been badly hit but the RAF tactic of targeting the bombers worked, even if they did so after most had attacked. Together with anti-aircraft guns, the RAF shot down a further eight bombers in addition to the two that were lost in the attack on Ventnor. In human terms, twenty-nine bomber aircrew were killed, seven taken prisoner and a further two wounded. Despite the bombing success, the loss of sixteen percent of the attacking force was sobering and the RAF's success against such overwhelming numbers must have been encouraging, as one Spitfire pilot noted:

Pilot Officer David Crook, 609 Squadron

"My God," I muttered to myself, "What a party." I was not the only person to be impressed. Several other people (not only in 609) who were also in this fight told me afterwards that their main impression had been one of blank astonishment at the numbers of aircraft involved. As somebody remarked "There was the whole German Air Force, bar Goering." Later in the summer, we got used to seeing these enormous formations but this first occasion certainly made us think a bit.

Despite the massive effort by *Luftflotte* 3, it was left to *Luftflotte* 2 to continue the day's fighting targeting the airfields of Manston, Hawkinge and Lympne, stretching the defences to the full. The day had seen the most intensive day's fighting so far in the Battle of Britain and, alarmingly, the RAF had seen a switch in the *Luftwaffe*'s aims to targets specifically involved with the air defence of the United Kingdom. If the RAF pilots had found 12 August 1940 hard work, many of the days that followed would be similarly hard.

At first light on 13 August, most of the German airfields commanded by *Luftflotte* 2 were hives of activity and then, between 0550 hrs and 0610 hrs, the first bombers lifted off into a cloud-laden sky. *Adlerangriff* had begun – a systematic attack against what the Germans thought were fighter airfields. However, the crews were not aware that because of the inclement weather, the attack had been postponed and just after they were airborne, the message was passed. However, only the fighter escort heard that the attack was cancelled and returned to base whilst the bombers droned onwards unaware that they were unprotected. To add further insult, a number of the airfields briefed to be attacked on this day did not belong to Fighter Command and, as a result, aircraft and lives would be lost and crews taken prisoner unnecessarily:

Oberleutnant Heinz Schlegel, *Stab*/KG 2

13 August 1940 was declared *Adlertag*. All of the *Luftwaffe* was to pounce on the RAF and destroy it on the ground as far as it was possible. KG 2 had been briefed to attack the RAF airfield at Eastchurch near the Thames Estuary. A *Zerstoerergeschwader* was to escort us and ensure our protection. As far as I remember, all three *Staffeln* of III *Gruppe* and the *Stabstaffel* took off from Arras at about 0600 hrs.

The *Geschwaderkommodore* was *Oberst* Johannes Fink. He was a conscientious officer – no daredevil. Before commanding KG 2, he had been responsible for the investigation of flying accidents at the *Reichsluftfahrtministerium*. There, he had very often seen accidents caused by ignoring flying orders (such as visiting relatives) and therefore he always fulfilled the orders given to him. He had the order to go to Eastchurch and so he went to Eastchurch.

The *Stabstaffel* was on its way with three aircraft: in the centre the *Kommodore*, my aircraft on his left, a little but higher and behind him.[2] If I can remember, this *Kette* was flying behind the rest of the *Geschwader*. Anyhow, in the very first plane was a *Staffelkapitaen* who was in radio contact with the *Kommodore* to receive further orders. The whole unit had switched to this wavelength which was the reason that nobody heard the attack had been cancelled because of bad weather. It was only possible to recall I *Gruppe*.

Different to normal missions, the *Staffelkapitaen Oblt* Osswald flew with us. He was always scared and only flew when it was unavoidable – like this day. Because he was convinced that nothing could happen

[2] The third aircraft in the *Stabstaffel* was flown by *Oblt* Hans Langer.

Oblt *Heinz Schlegel (left). To his left are unidentified,* Ofw *Ernst Holz and* Ofw *Gustav Babbe.* (Schlegel)

Oblt *Gerhard Osswald,* Staffelkapitaen *of*
Stabstaffel/*KG 2.* (Schlegel)

to me (I had been shot down in France during a low level reconnaissance flight), he climbed into my aircraft.

And so KG 2 (less I *Gruppe*) flew towards the Thames Estuary longing to see a *Zerstoerer* escort. After reaching the Channel, the formation flew into a thick layer of cloud. A single *Zerstoerer*, which presumably was there to draw our attention to the fact that the mission had been cancelled, circled us and disappeared again. It was obviously mistaken for our escort. When in our estimation we had reached the target, the clouds became thinner but the target could still not be seen so the formation flew in a wide turn towards London where we turned around again. Now the formation was on an easterly course. The airfield was spotted through a hole in the cloud which was at 800m height – we were flying at 1,500m. After flying another 180° turn, we attacked descending through this hole and dropped our bombs quite accurately. But then, the British fighters came from the east from the direction of the sea where the rising sun prevented us from seeing them. So, it came as a complete surprise when their salvoes hit us. Neither the *Bordfunker* nor the *Bordmechaniker* had a chance to shoot. Both were wounded, especially in their forearms. The aircraft was hit in the fuselage and in the engines. I succeeded in pulling the plane into the thin layer of cloud but soon the left then right engine seized.

Stab/KG 2 on an operational flight during the Battle of France. (Schlegel)

Damage to the 142 Sqn hangar at Eastchurch, 13 August 1940. (Gosman)

I realised that we could not fly back over the Channel again and I did not know if the wounded crew members could operate their parachutes so the only thing to do was to make a force landing. An open meadow appeared, or it seemed to be open, so was the obvious place. But, everywhere in southern Britain, the inhabitants had done things to prevent these meadows from being used by aircraft – ditches had been dug, earth piled up in ramparts and poles had been rammed into the ground so this friendly meadow turned out to be quite bumpy. The aircraft landed heavily and came to a standstill at a big tree. After we had got out and had a look around, some unarmed soldiers appeared. They asked for our pistols – there was no way we could have conquered England with those pistols anyway!

All across southern England, *Luftwaffe* bombers roamed looking for targets – to the west, twenty Junkers 88s of I/KG 54 and a further eighteen from II/KG 54 headed for the airfields of Farnborough and Odiham; a further eighty-eight *Stukas* from StG 77 had their attack cancelled when they were half-way across the Channel. Again, as with previous attacks mounted by *Luftflotte* 3, there was a massive fighter escort but, again, it failed to prevent the RAF from harrying the bombers. The Germans did report attacking the two airfields but it would appear that little damage, if any, was caused. The cost to these attackers was four Junkers 88s shot down and a further nine

THIS AND NEXT PAGE Oblt *Schlegel's Do 17 after its enforced landing.* (via Cornwell)

Oblt Heinz Rose of Stab II/KG 54 is helped to captivity – his Ju 88 crashed into a lake near Arundel early in the morning of 13 August 1940. (via Hutton)

returning to France with varying degrees of damage. Again, the human cost was high – thirteen killed, six prisoners of war and four wounded. Added to the losses suffered by KG 2 – five bombers destroyed and seven damaged with eleven killed, nine prisoners of war and seven wounded – *Adlerangriff*'s false start had cost the German bomber crews dearly.

To make matters worse, later that afternoon another confusing series of attacks developed to the west. Targets this time were the airfields of Boscombe Down, Warmwell, Yeovil, Worthy Down, Andover and Middle Wallop using a mix of thirty-nine Junkers 88s from I and II/LG 1 and fifty-two *Stukas* from I/StG 1 and II/StG 2. A further sixty-one Junkers 88s and fifty-two *Stukas* of StG 3 were also briefed to attack airfields in the Portland area and Portland itself slightly later but, because of deteriorating weather, this was not carried out. Nevertheless, the two raids cost the *Luftwaffe* six *Stukas* from II/StG 2 and two Junkers 88s from III/LG 1 and again, despite reporting to have badly damaged Andover and Middle Wallop airfields and military and maritime targets in between and including Southampton and Bournemouth, very little damage was inflicted and what damage was done had no adverse impact on Fighter Command.

Adlertag's daylight attacks then switched back to the east, the daylight attacks ending with an unopposed attack on the airfield at Detling in Kent by twenty-six *Stukas* believed to be from IV/LG 1. In addition to the destruction of buildings, hangars and aircraft, in excess of sixty military and civilian personnel were killed, including the Station Commander. However, Detling did not figure in Fighter Command's order of battle and despite the personnel losses and severe damage to the airfield itself, the attack did not affect the RAF's ability to counter German air attacks.

So ended *Adlerangriff* – a day riddled with errors, miscalculations and misinformation from the German point of view. Following the Detling attack, a few *Luftwaffe* aircraft strayed over the United Kingdom and for the first time in a number of nights, nocturnal attacks were few and far between even though Heinkel 111s of KG 27 and KGr 100 attacked industrial targets as far north as Glasgow. The RAF could have done better throughout 13 August 1940 but the weather, earlier attacks on radar stations and the size and depth of attacks made things difficult, whilst what successes they achieved were further assisted by the *Luftwaffe*'s errors.

In comparison, 14 August 1940 was a much quieter day. At about lunchtime, *Erprobungsgruppe* 210 carried out an attack against the hard-hit Manston airfield, losing two Messerschmitt 110s to light anti-aircraft fire. Soon after that, a heavily escorted formation of *Stukas* from IV/LG 1 unsuccessfully attacked Hawkinge airfield and sank the Goodwin Lightship. The attacks that then occurred for the remainder of the day were undertaken by a number of units against a number of targets using the poor weather as a means of defence. The attacks were numerous and ranged far and wide. Seventeen Junkers 88s of I/LG 1 carried out an armed reconnaissance in the Bristol area and attacked a number of airfields in the south west of England; III/KG 55 carried out seven separate attacks against the airfields at Abingdon, Upavon, Bicester, Worthy Down, Netheravon and Brize Norton and the Rolls Royce factory at Crewe whilst I/KG 27 sent eighteen Heinkel 111s to attack the airfields at Little Rissington, Hullavington, Upavon, Netheravon, Boscombe Down and 'Minchinhampton' (presumably Aston Down). The final unit in action that afternoon was III/KG 27 which sent

Bomb damage to a hangar at Middle Wallop on 14 August 1940.

twenty-five Heinkel 111s to attack the airfields at Blandford Forum, Yeovilton, Filton and Sealand near Chester. For the defenders, it was a confusing series of attacks to defend against. However, I/LG 1 lost a Junkers 88 to a Spitfire of 234 Squadron and another from 609 Squadron whilst another of that unit's Junkers 88s was shot down by four Hurricanes from 43 Squadron. III/KG 27 lost five bombers to Spitfires from 92 Squadron and three Spitfires flown by instructors from Number 7 Operational Training Unit. The final loss was more serious for the *Luftwaffe* when the *Geschwaderkommodore* of KG 55, *Oberst* Alois Stoeckl, the Chief of Staff for V *Fliegerkorps*, *Oberst* Walter Frank and KG 55's navigation officer, *Oblt* Bruno Brossler were all killed when their Heinkel 111 was shot down by two Spitfires from 609 Squadron.

The remains of the aircraft that did it – Oblt *Wilhelm Heinrici's Ju 88 from 1/LG 1.*

German air attacks that night were much reduced and it was anticipated that Thursday 15 August 1940 would see air operations over the United Kingdom hampered again by bad weather. Apparently, the bad weather prompted *Reichsmarschall* Goering to summon his senior officers to Germany; these officers were destined not to witness first hand a day that the surviving German aircrew would call *Schwarzer Donnerstag* – Black Thursday.

One of the successful No.7 OTU pilots that shot down a He 111 of 8/KG 27 on 14 August 1940 was Fg Off Peter Ayerst.

Heinkel 115 (seen here from 1/706). (Rosenbaum)

German losses began early. A number of German aircraft, predominantly Heinkel 115 seaplanes, carried out mine-laying and attacks against airfields in north eastern Scotland. One of their number was dazzled by searchlights and flew into the ground near Arbroath at 0430 hrs.

As dawn broke, numerous German reconnaissance aircraft scurried along the south coast, *Oblt* Hans Horn's Dornier 17 P of 3(F)/31 having the misfortune to be shot down off the Isle of Wight at about 0800 hrs. However, the first full scale raid did not materialise until just before lunchtime when the airfields of Lympne and Hawkinge were attacked by *Stukas* from IV/LG 1. Both airfields were bombed but the intervention of RAF fighters managed to thwart much of the attack on Hawkinge (a fact confirmed by returning German crews) but Lympne was badly hit and was non-operational for the next two days. The German fighters inflicted casualties on the RAF fighters but did not prevent the loss of two *Stukas* – one was chased into high tension cables at Folkestone whilst the other came down off the coast:

Hauptmann **Rolf Muenchenhagen, 10***(Stuka)***/ LG 1**

We took off from Tramecourt under the lead of the *Gruppen Kommandeur, Hptm* Roeder. I was not the *Staffel Kapitaen* but was being trained as one; as a result, I had only been with the *Geschwader* for three days. About five miles from the English coast between Dover and Folkestone, we were attacked by Hurricanes. One Hurricane attacked me from behind (I was the last one in the *Staffel*) and he hit my *Stuka*. I was forced to bale out but on the way out, I myself was hit. As I went down, the Hurricane circled me. Just before I hit the water, I released myself from the parachute and I landed in the sea without any trouble. As I floated in the water, the Hurricane dived at me at intervals as if to show my position. Shortly afterwards, a patrol boat picked me up – the crew were very fair and they gave me cigarettes and covered me with a blanket. I was then landed at Dover and taken to a military hospital. I later found out that I had lost an eye and a number of teeth.

Hptm Muenchenhagen was a victim of a Hurricane of 501 Squadron. Who shot him down for certain cannot be said for sure but one pilot's combat report gives a good idea of what it was like shooting down a 10/LG 1 aircraft and could have been the pilot who circled the German pilot floating in the Channel:

Flying Officer Robert Dafforn, Green 2, 'B' Flight, 501 Squadron

Enemy aircraft were first sighted five miles south of Folkestone (twenty Ju 87s and six Me 109s[3]) heading towards Hawkinge. I singled out a Ju 87 and did a Number One attack from rather below (five seconds burst). Enemy aircraft started to smoke and dived away and I broke away. I was unable to see what happened to the enemy aircraft.

I then singled out another Ju 87 and did a Number One attack from dead astern. Eleven second burst from 300 yards gradually closing. Enemy aircraft started smoking and diving. I broke away but was unable to see what happened to the enemy aircraft. My ammunition was now exhausted but I noticed two pilots in the sea three miles south of Folkestone so I attracted the attention of a boat in Folkestone Harbour and then circled the two pilots. They were eventually picked up by Motor Torpedo Boats from Dover...[4]

As this raid was taking place in the south, the scene of battle was about to shift much further to the north. For the first time in the Battle of Britain, *Luftflotte* 5 was carrying out its first major attack. The targets were the airfields of Dishforth and Linton-on-Ouse in Yorkshire (both bomber airfields) with secondary targets being harbours along the north eastern coast. The dubious honour of carrying out this attack went to the Heinkel 111s of I and III/KG 26 based in Norway:

---

[3] There were considerably more than six Messerschmitt 109s as the escort was made up from various *Gruppen* from JG 26 and JG 51.
[4] There were at least three RAF pilots in the water at that time – Sgt Norman Lawrence of 54 Sqn and Flt Lt Alan Putt and Fg Off John Gibson of 501 Sqn.

Oberleutnant Hermann Riedel, 8/KG 26

Tension began to build before 14 August 1940 indicating that we were in for some action. Then the order arrived to prepare for an attack on Britain. It was said that the British fighter defences were reduced to about thirty or forty aircraft. Therefore a simultaneous attack on airfields in the south and the north would have a crippling effect.

Oblt *Hermann Riedel (right) with* Fw *Willi Scholl.* (Riedel)

KG 26 was briefed to meet over Stavanger and attack in close formation. Up to a certain point escort would be undertaken by Bf 109s from II/JG 77 and in the middle of the North Sea, I/ZG 76 would take over. I/ZG 76 was equipped with the Bf 110 with additional tanks. All preparations were made and then the attack was changed from 14 to 15 August.

The airfield at Stavanger was very busy. By 1100 hrs, everything was ready – crews in their aircraft, engines running. Slowly the *Ketten* and *Staffeln* taxied to the take off position. In the lead was the *Gruppen Kommandeur Maj* Guenther Wolfien. The *Ketten* took off in swift succession – *Staffel Kapitaen Hptm* Josef Stefan was in the lead *Kette* of 8/KG 26 – the leader of the port *Kette* was *Oblt* Horst von Besser; I was the leader of the starboard one. Climbing very slowly, we all closed up in tight formation.

'Vestigium Leonis' – mark of the lion and mark of KG 26.

Off the coast, I/KG 26 from Kristiansand appeared. We climbed slowly to 6,000m altitude. All around, the fighters from II/JG 77 capered reassuringly. After a while, the *Zerstoerers* appeared on both sides of the formation and the Bf 109s left for home.

As the final *Kette* on the starboard side, I had a splendid view up and down the vast formation. The Bf 110s held a steady course – some times they came closer, went on ahead or dropped back.

Radio silence was ordered for the duration of the flight. We had a Signals Officer who, it was said, could identify British pilots by their voices. He kept monitoring British radio traffic throughout the flight. However, about 100 kilometres from the coast, unintelligible warnings came over the radio and in no time, the formation became nervous. Over the radio and from my crew came warnings of enemy fighters and I observed several on reciprocal courses to ourselves. In a wide curve, they came in to the rear of the *Zerstoerers* and a glimpse to the right saw two Bf 110s falling in flames. The attack was swift but I did not see any of the bombers being attacked.

We followed our course undisturbed and crossed the coastline. A damaged *Zerstoerer*, so I was informed from the lower gun position, was trying to find protection from us but it soon disappeared. After crossing the coast, we should have changed course but we continued. Eventually, we turned south but clouds covered the airfields and in a wide turn, the *Gruppe* turned north east towards Newcastle where the city and harbour was clearly visible.[5] The harbour was our alternative target so we unloaded our bombs there. Reaching the sea, the *Gruppe* inexplicably turned left back towards the city and now, without warning, enemy fighters closed on the formation and attacked.

My aircraft was immediately under heavy fire. The bullets, like rain, passed my head left and right and into the instrument panel. We were just about able to keep formation when, over the city, we were attacked again. The starboard engine broke down with a jolt and began to burn. A Spitfire then flew alongside – the pilot waved his hand and then disappeared. He was obviously out of ammunition and wished us good luck!

As I was not able to keep formation and had to extinguish the engine fire, I dropped away from our disintegrating formation and headed east. The clouds were now broken but I managed to level off in a cloud bank and set course for Holland. The aircraft was in a

Two other crew members, Ofw Kalle Mueller (left) and Ofw Paul Suessenbach (right), inspect damage to their He 111 received over Narvik with another unidentified crew member. (Riedel)

[5] It is believed that Sunderland not Newcastle was the city seen as it was the former that was bombed.

shambles both inside and out. The fire had gone out and the port
engine seemed to be running normally but nearly all the instruments
were destroyed. Amazingly, all the crew were uninjured but there was
quite a tension in the aircraft. We were determined to reach safety. My
Beobachter Fw Willi Scholl calculated the straightest course whilst the
Bordfunker, Ofw Paul Suessenbach, tried to contact a ground station.
He was lucky and managed to transmit a distress message despite
much confusion over the radio frequency.

We checked all parts of the aircraft very carefully especially the
still running engine. Our height by now was only some 1,000m
above the sea and after some time had passed, we were startled by
rough noises coming from the port engine. One of the still working
instruments showed that the oil temperature was rising and I had to
throttle back. We slowed right down and started losing height.
Keeping the aircraft in a shallow glide, I tried to keep going but
then the oil temperature suddenly shot up, the engine began to
smoke and with a shudder, it broke down. Height was now just
200–300m, enough time to prepare for ditching. The dinghy was
ready and everybody tightened their seat belts and gliding down,
with the flaps slightly down, we touched the waves.

All of a sudden, water was all around – dark and tasting very salty!
Then slowly, it got quieter and we saw some light – we were afloat. We
threw off the roof hatch, left the aircraft and got into the dinghy. To
save weight, we only took the emergency rations pack. Boarding the
dinghy last, I remembered my cine camera. With a jump, Kalle
Mueller [*Ofw* Kalle Mueller, the *Bordmechaniker*] returned to the cockpit
and came back with it – quite a feat in the rough sea! Unfortunately, all
the flight documents and exposed films had to be left in the cockpit.

It was all quiet in the
dinghy. We drifted fast,
moving away from the
pitching aircraft. The
dinghy drifted like a leaf on
the wind and it was
impossible to steer by
paddles or sail. Minutes
later, the starboard wing and
nose of the Heinkel dipped
forwards and the plane
disappeared, the tail being
the last to say goodbye…

For *Oblt* Riedel and his crew,
rescue was on its way but their
adventures that day were not

Oblt Riedel's He 111 slips beneath the waves. (Riedel)

He 111s of I/KG 26 during the Narvik Campaign. (Kull)

destined to end there as the reader will see later.

III/KG 26 had suffered badly – 8/KG 26 had lost five aircraft whilst 9/KG 26 had the misfortune of running into three Bristol Blenheims from 235 Sqn who were on a sweep of the Danish coast. Two He 111s were immediately shot down – one by Plt Off Norman Jackson-Smith, the other being shared between Jackson-Smith, Plt Off John Laughlin and Sgt P. F. Hall. I/KG 26 was lucky to lose just one bomber:

Flieger **Ernst Henrichsen, 1/KG 26**

About 60 miles from the coast, we were joined by Bf 110s. Shortly afterwards, the warning 'enemy fighters' was given. The Bf 110s were engaged at once and I could see how one Hurricane attacked by a Bf 110 exploded into an orange fireball. The Bf 110 was at once attacked by a Hurricane and went down with smoking engines. Seconds later, this Hurricane exploded, just like the first.[6] After that, the dogfights went further away. I could see planes going down but could not see if they were friend or foe.

He 111s of 1/KG 26 in formation over the North Sea. (Machalett)

[6] Only one Hurricane was lost during the whole combat.

It all became quiet again and we reached the coast where we were welcomed by anti-aircraft fire. The shells exploded quite near and I could see the clouds of the explosions touch the wings of our plane. After crossing the coast, we flew on westwards for quite a time. I could hear some comments on the network like "What is going on?" and "Has the old man lost his way?" and so on. This suspicion was confirmed when I saw that we were over the sea again, apparently the Irish Sea and I saw what I thought was the Isle of Man. Then we turned around and crossed England a second time.

Nothing happened until we reached the coast again where we got the order to attack port facilities and warehouses. In order to do this, we had to break up our tight formation and during the following bomb run, we became dispersed. After our bombs had gone (I did not see if we had hit anything), I heard *Oblt* Roch telling the pilot *Uffz* Zimmermann "Flieg schneller! Den letzten beissen die Hunde!" ("Fly faster! The last [one] gets bitten by the dog!") He was right about that, for at the same time I saw Hurricanes were coming. There being no fighter escort any more, we were now attacked. They used a very prudent tactic. They attacked right from behind and shot at us from a distance of 1,500ft. At this distance, our single machine gun and inferior aiming were no match for the combined fire power of the Hurricane. Soon both engines were out of commission having been hit in the cooling system. Moreover, the three rear gunners were wounded – the upper rear gunner (*Gefr* Kulick) in the head, the lower rear gunner (*Gefr* Machalett) in the knee (with a broken leg) and I was hit by shrapnel in the upper and right side of the head. I had the feeling that someone had hit me over the head with a big stick! Then I could not see anything – I tried to wipe my eyes, could see again and saw that my hands were full of blood. For the first time, I realised that I had been wounded. This fighter attack took some time and we were by then back out to sea so the pilot turned back towards the coast and glided towards it.

At this time, the Hurricane stopped shooting at us. We were escorted up until the time the pilot ditched the plane. When we hit the water, the lower hatch opened and the sea entered the plane. In seconds, we were half full of water. I went back to

Gefr *Alwin Machalett in front of the He 111 in which he was shot down on 15 August 1940.* (Machalett)

help the lower rear gunner and while doing this I had a look at the newly installed armour plating – it was criss-crossed by rows of impacts by bullets just where I had been standing during the attack. However, we left the plane, inflated the dinghy and just about got away from the plane before it sank. About two hours later, we were taken aboard a trawler and made prisoners of war…

The RAF claimed forty-four Heinkel 111s and Messerschmitt 110s destroyed and it is difficult to tie RAF claims to German losses although it is believed that Australian Plt Off William Millington of 79 Squadron, who claimed three Heinkel 111s destroyed in this action, was responsible for shooting down the 1/KG 26 bomber.

Plt Off William Millington in the cockpit of his Hurricane after he had joined 249 Sqn; he was reported missing in action on 30 October 1940.

As an example, the following report gives an idea of what many of the RAF pilots experienced on that day:

Flight Lieutenant Forgave Smith, 72 Squadron

We started that day with our take off at about 1230 hrs with the Squadron of eleven Spitfires in three sections led by Flt Lt Ted Graham. As 'A' Flt Commander, I led one of those sections consisting Plt Offs Holland and Deacon-Elliott and, I think, Sgt Douthwaite. It was very unusual at that time for more than a flight to be at readiness. We flew due east, out to sea and at about 40 miles from the coast encountered a large formation of enemy bombers flying in close formation, escorted by Me 110s. At the time, due to our inexperience, we thought that the bombers were Ju 88s but they were in fact He 111s.

Upon sighting the enemy aircraft, Ted Graham gave the order to attack and I put my Section into echelon port. As it was not possible to turn into the attack quickly enough in that formation, I ordered a change to echelon starboard. As Deacon-Elliott crossed behind 'Dutch' Holland, it was thought by 'Dutch' that he was being attacked by Me 110s and he and Deacon engaged in a lively private battle!

I selected one of the bombers and attacked it from astern, firing at the starboard engine from which large pieces broke away. I turned away and attacked another He 111 causing smoke to stream from the port engine. I then attacked a third He 111 and could see the explosive 'De Wilde' ammunition flashing on contact. I pressed the attack very closely, firing directly into the fuselage. Presumably a bomb detonated and the aircraft exploded in a huge ball of flame which I narrowly avoided flying into. Breaking away, an Me 110 was approaching head on and I gave him a quick burst before running out of ammunition. During the engagement, the Me 110s flew in defensive circles.

On the day of the attack, there was a thin layer of unbroken cloud at about 10,000–12,000ft. This was very fortunate for Newcastle as the bombers which penetrated inland were unable to see the densely populated cities along the Tyne which probably saved them from serious damage.

After landing at Acklington, I quickly refuelled and rearmed and reported and then took off again alone and flew south along the coast to try and make contact but was not successful and returned to base.

If he had continued further south, he would have found himself intercepting another raid. This was an attack on another bomber airfield, that of Driffield near Bridlington in Yorkshire, by Junkers 88s from KG 30:

Unteroffizier Werner Evers, 7/KG 30

We had been at Aalborg in Denmark for about two months. It was a very quiet time with some flights to Great Britain such as the Rolls Royce factory. On 15 August 1940, the whole *Geschwader* took off from Aalborg for Great Britain. I do not remember the target but at that time targets were only military places or factories. We had the newest Ju 88 which was the fastest so we started last. As we reached the British coast, the Spitfires [sic] were waiting and they came in from behind, attacking the last aircraft. So, they started on us with success. One engine had no oil, the other no oil or coolant but we were still airborne. Our *Bordfunker* was dead (we did not know this but he had stopped shooting). The pilot, *Oblt* Bachmann, and myself tried to figure out what to do next and best. We could either try flying along the coast southwards for France but thought that we couldn't make it and so decided to fly over Britain to try and reach Eire, not to become prisoners of war but to be interned.

However, after we returned from the sea to the land, another Spitfire was on our tail and started shooting immediately. We had no chance to escape and I tried to throw off the cockpit roof to jump out by parachute. The roof came off immediately and all papers, cards etc flew out. When we were in a prisoner of war camp, we were visited by the Spitfire pilot who shot us down and learned from him that he thought after we lost our roof and he saw all the flying papers, that we had surrendered and he stopped shooting.

Uffz Werner Evers a few days before he was shot down. (Evers)

As we had lost height, we decided to crash-land. Bachmann already had experience of crash-landing. We looked for a wheat field but before that we jettisoned our bombs. The landing was successful and the aircraft didn't catch fire. We thought that the gunner *Flg* Walther must have been killed as he was in the belly of the aircraft and was lying there when we touched down. Anyone who knows the Ju 88 wouldn't

Werner Evers' Ju 88 on show somewhere in the UK in November 1940. (via Cornwell)

believe that he survived. We noticed that *Fw* Henneske was dead (shot in the head). Bachmann and myself had to pull him out of his seat as it was stopping Walther from getting out. We had orders to set the Ju 88 on fire but we couldn't as we were soon taken prisoner. As we still had our pistols, we were scared that we might get shot but I spoke some English and handed them over...

The two RAF Squadrons that intercepted this attack managed to shoot down eight Junkers 88s and badly damaged a further three. The German bombers did manage to drop 169 bombs on the airfield, killing thirteen personnel, wounding countless others and causing extensive damage to the airfield. Numerous building were damaged and destroyed including all five hangars. The attack also resulted in the destruction of eleven Armstrong Whitworth Whitley bombers but yet again, this airfield and those aircraft were not part of the air defence of Great Britain.

Luftflotte 5 had been taught a painful lesson and never again attempted such a major daylight attack. For the *Luftwaffe*, it clearly proved that there was no detectable weakness to the RAF's defences and, contrary to what propaganda was saying, the RAF was not down to its last forty fighters.

Now the scene of battle shifted back to the south with *Erprobungsgruppe* 210 carrying out its first attack of the day against the airfield of Martlesham Heath closely followed by attacks on the airfields at Eastchurch, Hornchurch, Rochester and Gravesend by Dornier 17s of KG 2 and KG 3. Milling about this massive formation was an equally massive formation of escorting fighters which allowed the attackers

Sgt Alexander McNay, Flt Lt Reg Lovett and Sgt John Brimble of 73 Sqn show off trophies from the Ju 88 of 3/KG 30 shot down near Bridlington; all three pilots would be dead within a month.

to successfully bomb Rochester and Eastchurch but KG 3 lost two bombers in the process with a further six returning with varying degrees of damage and wounded crew members.

Again, as this raid turned for home, another was appearing to the west. Twelve Junkers 88s of I/LG 1 were heading for the airfield of Andover whilst a further fifteen from II/LG 1 were heading for Worthy Down. Simultaneously to the west, twenty-seven *Stukas* from I/StG 1 and twenty from II/StG 2 would attack Portland, hopefully splitting the fighter defences. Unfortunately for many of those Germans involved, this ruse did not work and in any case the two airfields were, yet again, not Fighter Command airfields. Almost immediately after sweeping in over Selsey Bill, the Junkers 88s were attacked by Hurricanes of 32, 43, 111 and 601 Squadrons:

Unteroffizier Otto Rezeppa, 4/LG 1

We took off from Orléans–Bricy on the evening of 15 August 1940 and orbited waiting to form up. Our target was an airfield north of Winchester. Over St Omer, we picked up our escort of Bf 109s and in the distance to the west we could see the Bf 110s.

I flew in the aircraft that was the furthest right in the formation. Another aircraft in our *Kette* was flown by *Uffz* Erwin Poggensee.

Uffz *Otto Rezeppa.* (Rezeppa)

After we crossed the coast, I was the first to spot the enemy. I shouted and fired in the direction of the fighters as they swept in from the right. In what seemed a few seconds but was probably ten minutes, everything happened. We shot at a Hurricane on the tail of *Oblt* Hans-Joachim Helbig's aircraft (he was our *Staffel Kapitaen*). Suddenly, the *Beobachter*, *Uffz* Willi Rimek, panicked and jettisoned the cockpit roof and my gun. He then collapsed and lay on the cockpit floor with his mouth wide open – he had been shot in the back of the head and killed instantly. I then waved my handkerchief at the attacking Hurricane and *Uffz* Fritz Dieter decided to crash-land which he did at very high speed in a corn field. As the aircraft stopped, we all got out. I was limping – I had been shot in the right leg. We dragged out Willi's body just as British soldiers arrived and we all stood there, covered in dust. They took my camera, gun and knife and took me away from the aircraft on a stretcher. We were then taken to a hospital in Chichester where I met an RAF pilot who had a wound in his shoulder. He said I was lucky as I would survive the war – he was not sure he would.

Uffz *Willi Rimek and* Uffz *Fritz Dieter in front of the Ju 88 that they were flying on 15 August 1940.* (Rezeppa)

The RAF pilot who shot down *Uffz* Rezeppa's aircraft did not witness any of the dramatic events in the aircraft as his very terse combat report shows:

Flight Lieutenant Stanley Connors, Green 1, 111 Squadron

An initial attack was blocked by twelve Me 109s. I then selected

Otto Rezeppa's Ju 88 lying in a West Sussex field. (via Cornwell)

Flt Lt Stanley Connors of 111 Sqn.
(Morgan)

another Ju 88 and carried out a quarter and astern attack. Bits fell off the port engine and the starboard smoked badly. Aircraft glided down and force-landed. I watched the crew surrender to farm workers who ran up to the machine.

Meanwhile, other Junkers 88s from II/LG 1 had managed to get further inland but for another five crews their destiny was not to return to France, as one of them recalls:

Feldwebel Willi Lueder, *Stab* II/LG 1

Fw *Willi Lueder (left) and two unidentified personnel of III/KG 3.*

We could see the Isle of Wight when the circus started and the fighters were engaged in fights with Spitfires [sic]. Anyway, everything happened very quickly – there were losses on both sides and we saw many aircraft going down in flames. Suddenly, Hurricanes descended on us and hit us in the starboard engine. We left the formation – the smoke made breathing in the cockpit impossible and we could not hold the aircraft any longer. We jettisoned the bombs as we wanted to crash-land. Suddenly, the pilot gave us the order to bale out. I was the first to go, *Ofw* Heinz Grund followed. As we were dangling on our parachutes, we were circled by a welcoming committee of two Hurricanes...

Sergeant Leonard Guy, Red 3, 'A' Flight, 601 Squadron

I followed Red Leader [Flt Lt Archibald Hope] into the engagement but broke away after one short burst at an enemy aircraft from the beam. I then saw a Ju 88 being attacked by a Hurricane. I dived to join the attack and delivered several short bursts from astern and one from underneath. Black smoke was pouring from the starboard engine. During these attacks, enemy aircraft had lost height from about 15,000ft to 5,000ft. Then one airman jumped and landed safely and about a minute later, a second landed by parachute. Enemy aircraft continued to lose height very slowly and crash-landed in a field north-west of Petersfield. Flt Lt Hope was in the other Hurricane attacking enemy aircraft and witnessed its destruction. It crash-landed 200 yards from a second enemy aircraft which was on fire; Fg Off Davis (Yellow 1, 'A' Flt) was circling this blazing machine.[7]

Flight Lieutenant Archibald Hope, 'A' Flight, 601 Squadron

My logbook shows that we took off from Tangmere at 1705 hrs which presumably would have been local time because the rule that all flying times were recorded in GMT was not introduced until 1944. I was leading eleven aircraft of 601 Sqn flying in my usual Hurricane coded UP-P. We were ordered to patrol base and then I see that I

---

[7] The burning Ju 88 was probably from 5/LG 1 – *Fw* Herbert Pauck and his crew remain missing to this day.

recorded the height as 19,000ft. I think that this was the maximum height reached during the flight which lasted an hour. My logbook then reads "Found twelve Ju 88s and attacked them over Bishops Waltham. Beam and two stern attacks on main formation. One damaged then forced down with Sgt Guy near West Meon after firing at engines. Three parachutes. John McGrath and Mouse Cleaver wounded."

After circling around for what seemed a long time, because I was out of ammunition, the parachutes emerged and then the Ju 88 seemed to make a semi-controlled landing in a field just west or just south of quite a major road. It hit the near side of a hedge and then slid on its belly for about 25–50 yards. There was no fire.

Willi Lueder's Ju 88 creating much interest amongst the local populace. (via Hutton)

At the time, responsibility for the crashed aircraft was with Tangmere and I asked the Adjutant, Flt Lt Thompson, to see if he could get me the pilot's Mauser pistol. He could not get the pistol but he did give me the pilot's throat microphone.

Feldwebel Willi Lueder

...We landed in a meadow about 400m apart. My first thought was "There goes my leave!" because two days later I was to have gone on eight days leave. Instead I got myself six and a half years as a prisoner of war!

After about ten minutes, four Home Guard turned up and called from far away "Hands Up!" I didn't because I had landed rather heavily on my backside and had got myself a lot of bruises. I thought how I could make contact so I called "You have a cigarette for me?" "Yes, yes!" – the shotgun was pointed downwards and the question as to whether I was wounded were the signs between us. I handed them my pistol and gravity knife as a souvenir for what good would they have been to me? For me, the war was over.

All but one of these II/LG 1 were taken prisoner on 15 August 1940; a further eleven aircrew were killed. Back (l to r): Ofw *Willi Lueder* (Stab *II),* Fw *Horst Burkhardt (4/LG 1),* Ofw *Heinz Dittmann (4/LG 1),* Oblt *Pit Stuetzel* (Stab *II, POW 17 September 1940),* Ofw *Heinz Grund* (Stab *II),* Fw *Otto Rezeppa (4/LG 1),* Fw *Fritz Dieter (4/LG 1). Front:* Fw *Erwin Kusche (4/LG 1),* Ofw *Willi Richter (4/LG 1),* Fw *Willi Mueller (4/LG 1),* Fw *Erwin Poggensee (4/LG 1) (missing* Fw *Kurt Weigang* and Oblt *Stephan Suin de Boutemard* (Stab *II).*

Both I and II/LG 1 made it to their targets, even if I/LG 1 bombed Middle Wallop instead of Andover (Middle Wallop being a fighter airfield but the Germans appear not to have known that). One of the fleeing II/LG 1 aircraft also managed to bomb Tangmere but without any detriment to the airfield. Meanwhile, to the west, the RAF fighters were mauling the *Stukas* and their escort, accounting for four dive bombers; damage to Portland was reported as being negligible.

A Do 17 Z of KG 76. (Moll)

Luckily for the *Luftwaffe*, the day was coming to a close but before night fell, more bombers and lives would be lost. Dornier 17s of I/KG 76 were to attack Kenley but confused Croydon, Biggin Hill and Redhill airfields, ending up bombing what they thought was Biggin Hill but was in fact West Malling! At the same time, III/KG 76 was briefed to attack Redhill, the Messerschmitt 110 fighter-bombers of *Erprobungsgruppe* 210 carried out what has become one of the most well known if not controversial raids of the Battle of Britain. Briefed to attack Kenley, they in fact bombed Croydon airfield a few more miles further north. Although they succeeded in hitting the airfield (and, by mistake, civilian housing just outside the perimeter), they were pounced upon by at least three Hurricane squadrons.

Six Messerschmitt 110s were shot down fleeing for the coast as well as an escorting Messerschmitt 109 from 3/*Erprobungsgruppe* 210. The *Gruppen Kommandeur*, *Hptm* Walter Rubensdorfer, was one of those who failed to

Two of the ErprGr 210 *fighter-bombers landed intact on 15 August 1940 – this one was flown by* Oblt *Karl-Heinz Koch.* (via Saunders)

return. If he had, perhaps he would have had to incur the wrath of his senior officers for bombing the wrong target and, more importantly, the London suburbs. Instead, he and his *Bordfunker* were killed; four days later he was posthumously awarded the *Ritterkreuz*. All of this was of little interest to the RAF pilot responsible for shooting him down; for him, it was just another incident at the end of a very busy day:

Pilot Officer Ron Duckenfield, 501 Squadron

On 15 August 1940, we were operating from Gravesend. In the afternoon, we were sent up to intercept a raid of about twenty Do 17s of which I claimed one damaged (over Detling). Then at about tea-time, just after we had refuelled, there was a much larger raid. This headed for Croydon and inflicted severe damage not only on the airfield but also on the town itself.

The scramble was given a little late so it was not until the enemy had actually finished his attack that we began to close. In the subsequent mêlée, the enemy formation having been broken by attacks from other RAF fighters, I suddenly found a Do 215 [sic] heading south in a long shallow dive towards the coast which gave him such a turn of speed that it took me some minutes before I could come near enough to open fire. I fired several bursts with no apparent effect (he was weaving pretty violently) but then, we were both down to about 4,000ft, I managed to hit him with the last of my ammunition. One engine caught fire and there must have also been a casualty in the cockpit because he rolled over and dived into the ground somewhere just west of Tunbridge Wells. I had no time to check exactly where because I was already very low on petrol.

Darkness now fell and the *Luftwaffe*'s nocturnal bombers set forth. The RAF had survived its first major test and had taught the *Luftwaffe* not to underestimate its strengths wherever they might attack in Great Britain. For those crews fortunate to make it back to their bases on the Continent, the loss of so many aircraft and personnel must have been sobering. However, for one German crew the day was by no means over and their misfortune was set to continue. Shot down during the *Luftflotte* 5 attack on the north of England, one German bomber crew was still adrift in the North Sea:

Oberleutnant Hermann Riedel, 8/KG 26

To soothe our nerves, we calculated our position and how long it would take to cross the North Sea. We thought that we were close to the British coast so refrained from shooting off flares – we were not set to become prisoners of war. The high waves gave us no end of trouble and after a while, some of us were affected by sea sickness. Conversation was sparse and as the day turned into evening, we began to lose hope of being rescued – Paul's [*Ofw* Paul Suessenbach] nerves gave way and he got the blues.

Then, from the south, in spite of the slapping of the waves, we heard the sound of an aircraft engine. A speck appeared to the south east which turned out to be a seaplane. We waited to be sure of the type and, when we clearly identified a Heinkel 59 [from *Seenotstaffel* IV, Norderney], we promptly shot off our distress flares. We had to wait a few anxious minutes before we saw the plane had spotted us. In a wide curve, it returned, crossed over us and prepared to land. I could hardly believe that the plane would be able to land on those waves and after several attempts, it touched down near to our dinghy. Again and again, the Heinkel disappeared behind mountains of water until at last the crew could throw us a hook. I still cannot remember how we managed to get on board the seaplane. We were dragged through an open hatch in the rear, brought forward and sat down. The dinghy was taken in and left in the back. At once the pilot tried to take off – this seemed to me to be the most difficult and longest take-off of my life.

The seaplane rocked like mad, increased its speed, slapped back into the water and just would not gain height. It seemed to be burying itself into the waves. In the cockpit, I could see the legs of the pilot, water and froth and how the pilot was struggling with his aircraft. After a long time, the banging in the plane and the rumbling engines quietened down – we were obviously in the air. This was an even greater relief to us than the end of the fighter attack.

Once in the air, my crew were dried and taken care of. We received dry underwear, track suits and blankets. My men then made themselves comfortable in the cabin. I introduced myself to the commander (the *Beobachter*) and the pilot. The pilot was busy but informed me that we were headed for Heligoland. The commander was a *Leutnant zur See* [Siegfried Boerner] and had only recently trained to be a *Beobachter*. He told me that there had been many distress calls during the afternoon and was not sure how close he was to the British coast as he had lost his bearings.

In the meantime, it was now night. I lingered a while with the pilot (he was an old hand). The *Beobachter* was in the open forward observation position. I joined him later – we had a clear night sky, flying above the clouds. Back in the cockpit, I noticed the *Bordfunker* operating his Morse lamp so I went to find out what he was signalling to. On arriving at where he was standing, a look to the rear made my blood freeze. Not more than 50m above and behind hung a Wellington [sic] and it was following us.

I yelled to the *Beobachter* "That is a British aircraft!" and hurried as fast as I could into the cockpit. "Down into the clouds! It's an enemy bomber!" I shouted to the pilot. "Oh no..." he replied "...It is a German long range night fighter patrolling around here." "Down into the clouds!" I yelled again "They are going to attack immediately!" I couldn't get him to change height and then the bullets rattled into our aircraft. I jumped down and shouted to my crew to take cover behind boxes and bundles. Meanwhile, the Wellington, swinging from one side to the other, covered us with sustained fire – the bullets came from everywhere. I noticed at once that the starboard engine was beginning to stutter and a look through the window showed the engine sprouting flames.

At long last, the pilot went down and with roll dived into the clouds, then levelling the aircraft. Slowly the plane lost height and soon force-landed on the sea. A few moments later, the enemy aircraft came in from behind and opened fire again. I ordered the dinghies be prepared and to get them in the water as I feared we would be bombed. The *Beobachter* then cried out and collapsed – he had been hit in the belly and was in great pain. The *Bordmechaniker* and I took care of him. After some time, the shooting stopped and an eerie stillness came over the aircraft...

The German seaplane had been detected by a Lockheed Hudson of 206 Squadron, not a Wellington as Hermann Riedel had thought. The following report was submitted on its return to base:

Aircraft 'V' of 206 Sqn sighted a He 59 on the surface of the sea with engines running at 2155 hrs. Enemy aircraft fired recognition signals of orange and red turning to green and then took off. 'V' began attack with starboard 'K' gun and continued with front gun and finished with side gun. Enemy aircraft was brought down onto the sea and was last seen on fire at 2230 hrs. Combat fought at 0–500ft and 1,700 rounds fired. Enemy aircraft reported as having good manoeuvrability and top speed was considered to be 125-knot.

Meanwhile, back on the surface of the North Sea, the two German crews had further problems:

Oberleutnant Hermann Riedel

...We were busy with the casualty. We wiped the wound and dressed it as best we could but couldn't do any more for him. We had no injections in the First Aid kit and in any case did not know how to use them.

The wounded man soon became semi-conscious. The aircraft wobbled in the high seas and tilted more and more to starboard. The *Bordfunker* tried to contact a coastal station but soon gave up – the radio was dead.

I then looked at my men and saw that they had bravely attacked the emergency rum rations. They were quite drunk. I had strictly rationed our rum after our first ditching and then handed it out after we had been picked up. I didn't know that our rescuers had also handed out some rum. Paul Suessenbach wanted to show off to his colleague and pottered about with the radio. "I'll show you how to raise the whole world!" he boasted. He too had no luck – the radio stayed dead.

The seaplane tilted more and more dangerously to starboard. We were convinced that it would capsize so I ordered my crew and the *Bordfunker* to get into the dinghies and to be ready to get away from the plane if it capsized. Three of us stayed on board. We secured a dinghy to the port float and clambered onto the port wing tip. We were convinced that we would be rescued at daybreak. The waves were still very high but the *Bordmechaniker* and I carried the now deceased *Leutnant* from the cockpit to the port float, securing him safely to ensure that we took him with us in case we had to get into the dinghy.

The night passed slowly and the weather got worse. During the night, the dinghies with the rest of the crew drifted away and despite working hard were not able to return to the seaplane. Very soon they were far away...

The nightmare for Hermann Riedel and the two crews was set to continue despite them surviving the night on the freezing North Sea. Meanwhile, as dawn broke on 16 August 1940, if the two Air Forces thought that there would be a let up in German attacks, they were sorely mistaken. The day would see yet more action but this time it would be confined to the southern part of Great Britain.

The first attacks manifested themselves mid to late morning when a series of 'rolling' raids took place against a number of airfields in Kent and Essex. However, just after lunchtime another German formation was again plotted approaching the Isle of Wight and this attack would prove the vulnerability of one of the *Luftwaffe*'s hitherto terrifying bombers.

Twenty-nine *Stukas* of I/StG 1 were briefed to attack Tangmere together with twenty-five from III/StG 2. Simultaneously, *Stab* and III/StG 1 would attack the Fleet Air Arm airfield of Lee-on-Solent and Ventnor radar station whilst twenty-two *Stukas* from I/StG 3 would attack Gosport airfield. The fighter escort was equally massive with a mix of 268 Messerschmitt 109s and Messerschmitt 110s. However, despite all this effort, only one of the three airfields, Tangmere, housed fighters and the *Luftwaffe* would, yet again, end up spending considerable nugatory effort against targets not related to air defence.

The RAF response had been to match the threat but was not able to prevent serious damage being inflicted on Tangmere. Every hangar was hit, as were most other buildings and a number of aircraft destroyed or damaged. Personnel casualties were inevitable – in the region of twenty killed and nearly fifty wounded. The *Stukas* also succeeded in bombing Lee on Solent and Portsmouth airfields but not as badly as Tangmere, and yet again Ventnor radar was put out of action for nearly a week. Destruction and damage could have been worse had not III/StG 2 been mauled to such an extent that four *Stukas* were shot down (all from 7/StG 2) and a further four returning with dead or wounded crew (one of the wounded being the *Gruppen Kommandeur*, *Hptm* Heinrich Bruecker) and their part in the attack was called off. I/StG 1 also suffered, losing five aircraft with five crew men killed and four being taken prisoner:

Unteroffizier Erich Koenig, 3/StG 2

At the end of June 1940, I joined the *Staffel*. The attack on Tangmere was my only one against the British mainland – all others were against convoys or patrol flights. On this day, *Fw* Rocktaeschel and I were flying in the *Kette* of *Oblt* Goetzpeter Vollmer, our *Staffel Kapitaen*. After dropping our bombs on Tangmere, I tried to get away from the attacking fighters by flying very low. Two fighters pursued me and attacked constantly. During the course of this chase, we received several hits. East of the Isle of Wight, our engine seized up. Before that, I had tried to gain height for a parachute jump but now we were too low to bale out and my badly wounded *Bordfunker* would not have managed it. There was not too much time to think. I shouted for him to unbuckle, then threw off the roof, unbuckled as well and was only just able to level the plane when we hit the water. Our aircraft turned over and we were hurled out.

The two British fighter aircraft had stayed with us to the end. They circled the spot where we had hit the sea and I can remember that one of the pilots waved when he saw us swimming in the water and then flew away towards the coast. I think he notified the British rescue service or the Royal Navy.

Lying on its back, the aircraft stayed afloat for a few minutes and then it sank. After I had resurfaced, I swam to the aircraft, opened the compressed air bottle in my life jacket and looked for my *Bordfunker*. He had surfaced near the plane as well. It could have been a great deal worse for me. My life jacket had been damaged and did not hold air but I had an airbed with me which I had always put on my parachute, filled with a little bit of air. The parachute and airbed had also been thrown out of the plane so I was able to use it like a life jacket. I tied myself to my *Bordfunker* so that we would not drift apart and after we had been in the water for some time, a British sea plane arrived, leading a speedboat to us. The boat's crew pulled us aboard and when they saw that we were both wounded, they waved the sea plane to land. We were then transferred to this aircraft, flown to an airfield and from there taken by ambulance to a hospital in Chichester.

A few times a Squadron Leader visited me in the hospital. From him, I learned that *Fw* Rocktaeschel and *Ofw* Witt had been killed during the attack on Tangmere. He also told me that from the logbooks which were found in *Ofw* Witt's briefcase, he knew that both had been old hands with many missions in Poland and France. *Ofw* Witt was responsible for keeping the logbooks in accordance with the rules. He had collected all the logbooks to check and sign them and he had taken his briefcase on this mission!

The battered remains of Fw Rocktaeschel's *Stuka – mortally wounded, he managed to land the aircraft.* (via Watkins)

The series of attacks, although achieving some success, had resulted in many lives lost and, in the case of III/StG 2, they had not even made it to the target. If the *Stuka* crews thought that 16 August 1940 was a bad day, worse would come in two days time.

Later in the afternoon of 16 August, a series of attacks, all against airfields from Benson in Oxfordshire in the west to Hornchurch in Essex in the east, stretched Fighter Command's resources to the limit. The major attack was by seventy-five Heinkel 111s from all three *Gruppe* of KG 55 against airfields at Heathrow, Heston and Feltham. Even this attack was not directed against fighter airfields and the Germans suffered four bombers destroyed, a further one damaged, ten crew killed, three taken prisoner and four wounded. However, one attack, again against a non-fighter airfield, had spectacular results when two Junkers 88s from an unknown unit carried out an audacious attack on Brize Norton in Oxfordshire. The result was that nearly fifty training aircraft were destroyed and countless others damaged.

Meanwhile, back in the North Sea, the two German crews, shot down over twenty-four hours before, were still struggling to survive:

Oberleutnant Hermann Riedel, 8/KG 26

Around noon on 16 August 1940, a seaplane appeared. It was an air sea rescue seaplane like ours – white with red crosses. It was a three engined Dornier 24[8]. It circled round us and prepared to land. With red signal flares and by waving our arms, we tried to make the pilot to go towards the drifting dinghies. The crew understood this and flew off north-east. We did not see anything of this plane for the rest of the day. We waited in vain.

In the afternoon, a ship appeared but remained at a certain distance. Nothing further happened that day – we were stiff from the cold, hungry and thirsty. We had some emergency rations but most of them were in the dinghies that had drifted away.

Early in the afternoon of the next day, we had drifted nearer to the ship. It had to be a German mine sweeper. Then a motor launch left the ship and crept nearer and with great difficulty tied up to the starboard float to take us on board.

The Do 24 arrives overhead. (Riedel)

[8] This was a Dornier 24 coded D-APDA of *Seenotflugkommando* 1 flown by *Oblt* Karl Born.

We had to stay on the wing tip until our
dead comrade was taken on board. This
was difficult and the boat was damaged
so much that the naval ratings went back
to the ship with great difficulty. Once
there, the motor launch sank!

It took a long time before a rowing
boat left the ship and reached our
seaplane. This one came to the port float
and we jumped on board. The oarsmen
pulled away and relieved of our weight,
the seaplane tilted to starboard and sank.

The minesweeper and help arrives. (Riedel)

The He 59 capsizes. (Riedel)

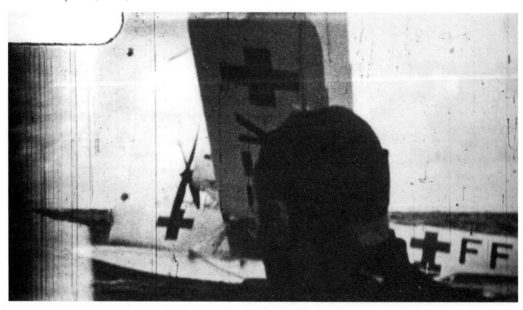

Once on board the ship, we received a hearty reception. We promptly
had a medical check up, a hot bath and dry clothes before being given a
bunk. I got up and made my way to the bridge and questioned the
Captain. From what I told him, he was able to make towards the other
dinghies and seaplane. The seaplane and the ship made radio contact
and we knew that all were safe and sound. As we neared the Do 24, we
could see all three engines hanging down from the wings.

The launch went out to bring the crews to the ship – thank God all were well. The day before, the Do 24 had found the dinghies but on landing in the rough seas, the three engines had broken from their mountings but the plane itself had remained seaworthy. I also learned from the Captain of the minesweeper that they had spotted us the day before but as we were in a minefield, they had not dared to come any closer!

The ship took the Do 24 in tow but near the entrance to Norderney Harbour, the seaplane, rocking dangerously, had to be cast off and sunk

by gunfire. Once in the harbour, our dead *LtzS* was carried ashore and we were taken to hospital. The next day I was able to fly a borrowed aircraft to KG 26's home airfield of Schwerin where I reported back. It was no surprise to learn that we were still reported as missing in action.

Despite the above dramatic events, German air operations for 17 August 1940 were almost non-existent and many might have hoped that 18 August 1940 would be similar. Apart from the usual reconnaissance flights, the first of three massive attacks on this day did not materialise until early in the afternoon.

The Do 24 under tow. (Riedel)

The burnt out remains of the only loss of KG 1 – Lt Rudolf Ahrens of I/KG 1 successfully crash-landed and then managed to destroy his He 111.

The first was aimed against the airfields at Biggin Hill, West Malling and Kenley by Heinkel 111s of KG 1 and Dornier 17s and Junkers 88s of KG 76. The attack on Kenley was a complex one consisting of high level attacks by all three *Gruppe* of KG 76 with 9/KG 76 finishing off with a low level attack. However, because of a delay over France and already alerted defences, the attack was not as successful as hoped. The same can be said about the attack by KG 1 which failed to cause any major damage to the airfield. The Germans lost nine bombers with a further ten damaged.

To add insult to injury, many of the bombers on this attack were carrying war reporters and cameramen (about eight in total) as well as a number of officers to gain experience. The most senior officer along for the attack, *Oberst Dr* Otto Sommer, was killed whilst one war reporter, *Sonderfuehrer* Walter Surk was killed and another captured:

Sonderfuehrer Willi Perchemeier

> On a magnificent day, we took off from our airfield at Creil. The target was Kenley aerodrome, the date 18 August 1940. It was intended that our *Staffel* would lure away the British fighters and *Flak* attention from another *Staffel* which would attack at low level. In addition, we would then dive-bomb the target. We flew at an altitude of 4,000m. A short time after the *Flak* stopped, the fighters appeared. One of them hit our port engine which immediately burst into flames. The fighter pilot had luck in so far as our gunner's machine gun jammed.
>
> There was no alternative other than to drop the bombs from high level rather than dive bombing and there was enough time afterwards to bale out. Unfortunately, our pilot could not get out of the plane in time and died an airman's death. Fear? Not at all – there hadn't been enough time; you just acted like a robot.
>
> Near the ground, hanging on my parachute, I tried to get past a threshing and harvesting machine but failed, landing between the tow bars and hurting my spine. I then dragged myself, limping, along the meadow until somebody from the Home Guard spotted and then arrested me. I was then taken away to a cell by car.

Much worse was about to occur to the west. The whole of StG 77 together with I/StG 3 were briefed to attack airfields in the Solent area. Twenty-eight *Stukas* from I *Gruppe* went for the Coastal Command airfield of Thorney Island, the same number of *Stukas* from II *Gruppe* targeted the Fleet Air Arm airfield at Ford whilst III *Gruppe*'s target was the radar station at Poling. Gosport airfield (which housed a torpedo development unit) was the target of I/StG 3. Again, the only target which had any relevance to the air defence of the United Kingdom was Poling. Although damage was inflicted on the airfields, especially Ford which was non-operational until September 1940, and Poling radar station which was put out of action for nearly a week, *Stuka* losses were nearly catastrophic. Ten *Stukas* from I/StG 77 were shot down and a further one written off on its return – seventeen aircrew, including the *Gruppen Kommandeur Hptm* Herbert Meisel were killed, five captured and six wounded. II *Gruppe* lost three aircraft, five men killed and one captured whilst III *Gruppe* lost one aircraft and one written off on its return and four men killed. Added to this, eight of the *Stuka's* escort were shot down whilst Fighter Command lost just five aircraft with two pilots killed and three wounded.

One more major attack would take place before dark. Dornier 17s of KG 2 aimed to attack Hornchurch airfield whilst the Heinkel 111s of KG 53 went for the airfield of North Weald. Eight RAF squadrons were scrambled to intercept both raids and their massive escort. However, both targets were obscured by cloud and the German bombers turned for home, dropping their bombs on coastal targets but not before four Heinkel 111s from KG 53, including one flown by the II *Gruppe Kommandeur*, *Maj* Reinhold Tamm, were shot down.

The Gruppen Kommandeur's *He 111 of II/KG 53, probably the same one flown by* Maj *Tamm on 18 August 1940.* (Hoehler)

Again, as night fell, the nocturnal bombers took to the air again, their crews probably relieved that they did not have to face Spitfires and Hurricanes. As for 18 August 1940, it stands out as the day in the Battle of Britain which saw the greatest number of aircraft destroyed or damaged on both sides. The *Luftwaffe* suffered sixty-nine aircraft damaged beyond repair or destroyed as opposed to the RAF's thirty-nine. However, the British lost a further twenty-nine, which were written off after being attacked on the ground. Furthermore, added to the losses suffered by the *Stukas* two days before, 18 August 1940 saw the end of Junkers 87 operations in the Battle of Britain. Yet again, thanks to correct tactics, courage and tenacity, Fighter Command had survived another test. For the *Luftwaffe*, criticism was heaped on the fighter *Geschwader* with the result that many of the *Geschwader* executive officers were replaced by younger, more aggressive men with specific orders to protect the bombers even closer. This was a blow to the Messerschmitt 109 and 110 pilots, especially the former, because on their *Freie Jagd* they were having greater successes over Fighter Command.

The next two days were virtually incident free. The only noteworthy incident being on 19 August when *Fw* Johann Moser of 7/KG 51 carried out another one of those audacious attacks against an airfield. This time it was the grass strip at Bibury in Gloucestershire, temporary home of 92 Squadron. One Spitfire was destroyed, another three damaged and one ground crew member killed. Two 92 Squadron Spitfires gave chase and shot the Junkers 88 into the sea but not before the Spitfire of Plt Off Trevor Wade had been damaged by return fire. He crash landed and managed to get clear of the Spitfire before it exploded; the four German crew were all killed.

21 August, however, saw the *Luftwaffe* taking advantage of the poor weather to undertake a number of *Stoerangriffe* or nuisance attacks. The first German loss occurred just before lunchtime:

Sonderfuehrer Kurt Rasche, attached to 2/KG 2

On 21 August, we had breakfast at our Officers' Mess – the mess being nothing more than an ordinary living room in a farmhouse. We were looking forward to our next trip into the town of Arras and as the cloud base was only as high as 300m, we didn't expect any flying. Nevertheless, we were ordered to take off – one aircraft only. We were to cause a little 'storm' on the other side – causing air raid alarms and, consequently, forcing people to hurry to the air raid shelters (especially, of course, the working population). The aircraft chosen was coded 'F' for 'Fritz', that is to say the one I regularly flew in.

Having taken off, we broke through the cloud but then reached another [layer]1,000m above the first one and broke through that one too and flew above the white cloudy sky in the sunshine. In the distance, we saw a British plane on a reciprocal course, possibly entrusted with orders similar to ours. Soon we guessed we were above

Sd Fhr *Kurt Rasche*. (Rasche)

England – a good reason to break back through the clouds. Finding ourselves still over water, we continued at that altitude and after a while we could see the land below us. Flying across woodland, we suddenly noticed a vast clearance and, under the trees near its edge, a big hangar. There was no question that this was a good object for our bombs. For this purpose, we turned back towards the hangar and dropped our bombs.[9]

A Do 17 Z of I/KG 2 practices an airfield attack.

Having not seen a single burst, we repeated our attack, flying towards the hangar. A second attack and we noticed nothing so we went into a dive. All at once, on the other side of the clearing, we discovered a number of military huts. At this moment we were certain that this was an airfield so we turned back to scrutinise in closer but this turned out to be once too much as suddenly one of the crew shouted "Spitfire!" They then attacked us from the flank – three Hurricanes…

[9] This was possibly Pulham airfield.

Sub-Lieutenant Richard Gardner, 'B' Flight, 242 Squadron

At 1200 hrs, 'Blue' Section [Flt Lt George Powell-Sheddon, Gardner and Plt Off John Latta] scrambled off its patrol line of Norwich. At 1210 hrs, we were given a vector of 190° followed by another of 240°. Enemy aircraft was sighted by the whole Section just off our port bow flying on a course of 270° magnetic. We were flying between two layers of intermittent cloud 8/10ths at 3,000ft. Enemy aircraft on sighting us dived in a left hand spiral showing the white crosses on his fuselage. Blue 1 got in a burst before enemy aircraft reached the cloud. Blue 2 and myself dived through the cloud after him. As I came out of the cloud, I found Blue 1 attacking again. I was unable to open fire. The enemy aircraft opened very heavy fire at Blue 1 as he closed in and broke away to the right.

I opened fire at 250 yards and concentrated on his port engine which caught alight. I then transferred my fire to his fuselage which also burst into flames after two seconds of fire. I closed to 20 yards. I stopped firing and followed enemy aircraft until he crashed in a wood.

Unteroffizier Heinz Hermsen, 2/KG 2

...As I was the *Bordfunker*, I was sitting with my back to the direction of flight and my duty was to pay attention to the rear. I did not realise what was going on at the front – I only noticed that something was wrong in the cockpit. When I turned my head, I saw fire and smoke. Now it was obvious – fighter attack! Then, three fighters appeared and attacked from behind. Over the intercom, I reported that we were under attack from behind but did not get an answer. Now, I had to repel the attacks and I think that one of the fighters had been hit because it showed a trail of smoke and turned to port. Because there was a short break in the attacks, I asked again what was going on but as before, there was no reply. Our entry hatch had gone and I couldn't see anyone...

Uffz *Heinz Hermsen*. (Hermsen)

Sonderfuehrer **Kurt Rasche**

...The long threads of their tracer approached our plane – immediately the port engine caught fire. I tried to defend ourselves by using the left hand machine gun. Ridiculous – what could I do with only one ammunition drum!

I felt that something had hit my legs. At that moment, the cockpit burst into flames. I couldn't see my comrades in the cockpit or the rear gunner and all at once, I was getting uneasy. I have no reason to be ashamed of admitting I was thoroughly frightened.

I tried to pull the red lever in the floor of the cabin for the door to drop away but I couldn't find the lever in the sea of flames. In fact, it was impossible to see anything at all. Suddenly, I realised that the cockpit roof had flown off and I tried to extricate myself upwards but in vain. The plane climbed and pressed me back but then it dived and I shot out quite by myself. I opened my parachute and landed in a meadow.

From afar, I heard dogs barking and a female voice getting closer and calling in German "Remain lying – we'll help you." Later a jeep arrived and took me to the camp we had just bombed. I was given immediate medical assistance and friendly attention. The Commanding Officer lent me his own pyjamas and later even his wife and child came to see me. In that camp, by the way, I came to know that our bombs had not exploded – our *Beobachter* had failed to arm them!

Unteroffizier **Heinz Hermsen**

...The plane was diving very fast and steeply towards the ground. Then there were critical moments. A new fighter attack. It was not possible for me to climb over my seat and bale out of the hatch. I had no choice but to pull the emergency lever and jettison the cockpit roof. Within seconds, the airstream blew the roof away which pulled me out of the aircraft. In my hand was the roof but not the ripcord. I had to feel for it and somehow I managed it. Looking back, I must say that I had been lucky because a few seconds after my parachute opened, I touched the ground. My watch said it was a few minutes to midday.

I met the *Beobachter* some time later – his hands were badly burnt. He told me that the pilot had been killed in the first attack and that his burns had been caused by an incendiary bomb and signal flares which exploded after this attack.

Dropping its cockpit together with the guns, the bomber continued flying northwards, missing a town hall clock by 50 feet. It then clipped a tree, crash-landed and careered across the ground at speed through a garden, killing two ponies, before it hit another tree and burst into flames. The charred remains of *Lt* Heinz Ermecke were buried five days later in the town into which the Dornier had almost crashed.

Less than an hour later, the next incident took place:

Sergeant Andrew Darling, Yellow 3, 'A' Flight, 611 Squadron

Yellow Section sighted the Do 17s flying inland at 4,000–5,000ft, speed 230–250 and in a tight 'V'. No evasive action taken by enemy aircraft before first attack. Yellow Leader [Sqn Ldr James McComb] ordered Number 3 attack and when in position to fire, I only got one burst at number three enemy aircraft as formation entered cloud. Immediately on picking up enemy aircraft for the second time, they again went into cloud. Before going in, I saw that number two enemy aircraft was pouring out smoke from starboard engine. I followed enemy aircraft, who were still in tight formation, into cloud and knowing I was close behind (because of the slipstream), gave another burst. Still in cloud, thick black smoke covered my windscreen and on coming out, I saw enemy aircraft hit ground and burst into flames. As enemy aircraft hit, I observed six or seven enemy descending by parachute.

Oberleutnant Herbert Schwartz, *Staffel Kapitaen* 6/KG 3

On 21 August, I had just returned from a training flight with two of the new aircrew when I learned that three planes each from 4 and 5 *Staffeln* had taken off for a mission. I got permission from the *Geschwader Kommodore* for a mission as well and decided to take the two new crews with me, thinking that this might be a good opportunity to get them acquainted with the real thing. In fact, both behaved very well flying out in cloud. Before we reached the British coast, we got word that we had been detected by radar. Still, this was no reason to abandon the mission. Unfortunately, leaving cloud to prepare for the attack, we found the Spitfires directly behind us and they had the good luck to silence my port engine. This meant abandoning the

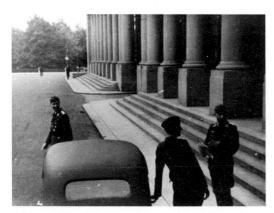

Left to right Oblt *Herbert Schwartz*, Lt *Guenther Zein (+29 August 1940) and* Oblt *Ulrich Matschoss, Brussels, July/August 1940.* (Dillen)

mission and returning home. As both the radio and intercom were out of action, I could only hope that the other crews would understand my change of course for Antwerp and disappearing into cloud again. Unfortunately, one of the aircraft [flown by *Uffz* Georg Pollmann] lost me in this manoeuvre and tried to find me again in the clouds which in fact he did but tearing off about two metres of the left wing and cutting deep into my fuselage, beheading the *Bordfunker* in the process.

The remains of Oblt *Schwartz's Do 17, 21 August 1940.*
(via Cornwell)

My plane went into spin and we were fast spiralling down. None of the usual manoeuvres could get the plane out of the spin and I decided to try the last resort – putting the plane onto its back. I didn't have to worry because the plane then broke up. As I gathered, the tail broke off, letting the fuselage flip upside down. My *Beobachter* broke through the cockpit roof and I must have got out the same way after my seat belt had broken. How the *Bordmechaniker* got out I do not know.

I only had to open my parachute and it was nice to hear the birds singing after all the noise of a few seconds before. In the distance, I counted four parachutes from the other aircraft and I still saw our adversaries flying around. I guess I came out at an altitude of about 400m because I landed very quickly. All of us were then rounded up by the personnel of a searchlight battery.

Oberleutnant Ulrich Matschoss, 6/KG 3

There is not much to add to the report of my pilot. I only remember that when we collided, I was pressed into the corner of the cockpit, unable to reach the handle for the emergency exit even though it was only a few inches from my extended arm. A movement of the plane threw me to the other side and I was then thrown forwards. I lost consciousness for a few seconds, woke up, saw my legs above me, then the earth, then my legs again and I thought it was high time to pull the handle of my parachute. I did so, it opened and I was then on the ground. Apparently the hole made by me when I was thrown out was also used by the rest of the crew.

Incidentally, that day I had caught a rather bad cold and was going to the medical station on the airfield when I met Herbert Schwartz who asked me to come with him on the mission. I said "I'm rather ill, I want to go to bed" and he said "You can lie down in two hours' time – we'll be back by then." It was seven years until we were back!

The foray by II/KG 3 was quite costly – in addition to the two Dornier 17s lost by 6 *Staffel*, Red Section of 611 Squadron also shot down two Dornier 17s from 4 *Staffel* flown by *Lt* Hellmut Krueger and *Fw* Max Zimmermann. This 'quiet' day had so far cost the *Luftwaffe* five Dornier 17s with ten aircrew killed and ten prisoners of war. The only RAF casualties were five Spitfires from 611 Squadron damaged in combat with II/KG 3.

Things then went quiet for a few hours before the *Luftwaffe* appeared over the now sporadically cloud laden British skies. This time, I and II/KG 54 took off to attack the airfields of Brize Norton and Abingdon and the Supermarine Factory at Southampton. The weather was both a blessing and a curse for the German crews as in addition to giving them protection, the targets were also to an extent protected. However, it didn't stop Red Section of 234 Squadron from shooting down *Ogefr* Gerhard Freude and his crew from 1/KG 54 – the aircraft crashed and exploded near Winchester: its crew are still listed as missing. Exactly two hours later, two of the II *Gruppe* aircraft briefed to attack the Supermarine Factory were intercepted by Hurricanes of 17 Squadron:

Oberfeldwebel Heinz Apollony, 4/KG 54

Briefing was at 1330 hrs, take off time about 1400 hrs. Fly singly from St André to Cherbourg, cross the Channel to Brighton, change course to London, from there change course to Bristol, change course to Southampton to drop high explosive incendiaries onto the Spitfire factory. Weather was supposed to be 8/10ths at 15,000ft. This would have been ideal weather for our mission but the moment we crossed the British coast, there were clear blue skies.

We decided not to fly the full course but to dive into Southampton and to get out as fast as possible. However, my *Bordfunker* must have been asleep because I saw the Hurricanes before he did and they were already diving towards us. All I could do was dump fuel which momentarily stopped the attack and gave me time to

Ofw *Heinz Apollony*. (Apollony)

Uffz *Kurt Miethner*, Bordfunker *in*
Ofw *Apollony's crew.* (Miethner)

release the bombs which fell into fields. Now I tried to outmanoeuvre the Hurricanes and to get back into the clouds over the Channel which I did successfully but the damage to the plane was too severe (both engines were overheating and losing power quickly whilst the dinghy was hanging in shreds behind the tail). It was therefore impossible to reach France.

I dropped out of clouds again – I knew that the Hurricanes would be waiting so the moment we came out, I released the canopy to show the pilots I was helpless and wanted to give up. This they accepted and stopped firing. Seeing a big enough field for an emergency landing, I came in for a good belly landing. Three minutes later we were taken prisoner.

Two Sections from 17 Squadron were scrambled to orbit their base at Tangmere. The first interception was by Blue Section from 'B' Flight:

Squadron Leader Cedric Williams, 17 Squadron

I was leading Blue Section [with Plt Off Harold Bird-Wilson and Plt Off Jack Ross] and was ordered to orbit base at 5,000ft at 1545 hrs. After being vectored to Worthing and return, an enemy aircraft was sighted 5 miles north-west of Tangmere just above cloud at 7,000ft. Enemy aircraft was then turning south. When the Section was about a mile away, enemy aircraft saw us and jettisoned bombs. I made a beam attack before enemy aircraft could reach cloud and he

THIS AND NEXT PAGE *Blue Section of 17 Sqn were quick to visit the scene of their kill, 21 August 1940.* (Bird-Wilson)

received some hits. On emerging, I did a second attack from slightly above and astern. Enemy aircraft then disappeared. On re-emerging, I saw Blue Two sitting behind it and firing. I waited a few seconds and made another beam to quarter attack. Spurts of flame were then seen to come from enemy aircraft which disappeared into cloud. It later crashed at East Wittering.

An hour later, Red Section accounted for the 4/KG 54 Junkers 88 of *Lt* Alfred Kiefer:

Flying Officer Count Manfred Czernin, 'A' Flight, 17 Squadron

Red Section [Czernin, Sgt Cliff Chew and Sgt Leonard Bartlett] was ordered to patrol base below clouds at 1645 hrs. Cloud was 8/10ths at 5,000ft. We were given three vectors before going above cloud. We were then over Beachy Head. On going above, I saw enemy aircraft at about 8,000ft and 3 miles away. I ordered Section into line astern and gave chase. Section delivered a stern attack and put rear gunner out of action. Enemy aircraft's speed at first seemed 250mph but after attack slowed down to 160mph. We then delivered three beam attacks; enemy aircraft took no avoiding action but was going down slowly. After fourth attack, enemy aircraft's starboard engine, which had then been smoking, burst into flames. Two crew thereupon jumped with their parachutes which opened and they landed in the sea. I then approached enemy aircraft which was still on an even keel although losing height. I saw behind the cross a red snake-like crest and in front the number 'B3' or '33'.[10] As we were then 20 miles south over the sea, I did not think it wise to follow enemy aircraft which was obviously going down.

The pain for the *Luftwaffe* did not finish there. Just before the above combat, Plt Off Ted Shipman leading Green Section of 41 Squadron (Plt Off Gerald Langley and Sgt Frank Usmar) shot down the Heinkel 111 flown by *Fw* Otto Henkel of 9/KG 53 into the sea 15 miles east of Scarborough – the crew of five (which included *Hptm* Georg Pfeiffer, *Staffel Kapitaen* of 9/KG 53) all perished. Then 238 Squadron shot down two Junkers 88s flown by *Uffz* Kurt Conrad and *Uffz* Jochen Hartmann of 2/KGr 806 following an attack on the airfield at St Eval in Cornwall. This unit, ostensibly trained to attack coastal targets and as such normally carried *Kriegsmarine Beobachters*, was apparently making its first appearance over the United Kingdom and lost eight aircrew for its troubles. Two more German bombers would be lost before midnight – *Lt* Konrad Ksienzyk and his crew from 8/KG 2 were shot down near Ipswich whilst on another nuisance raid and a 9/KG 30 Junkers 88 suffered engine failure during a nocturnal attack on the north of England and ditched just before midnight. The crews from these last two aircraft were taken prisoner.

21 August 1940 appeared a quiet day but proved the effectiveness of Fighter Command. Only one fighter was lost (catching fire and burning out after crash-landing) and that pilot slightly injured. The Germans lost thirteen bombers – in human terms, thirty-one men died and twenty-two were taken prisoner. If the days before 21 August had seen heavy losses resulting from considerable effort, this day saw even heavier losses resulting from a considerably reduced *Luftwaffe* effort.

The days that followed saw sporadic German bomber activity, not helped by the weather. On 22 August *Erprobungsgruppe* 210 put in two appearances, attacking a convoy code named TOTEM off Dover and then Manston airfield. 23 August was even quieter than the days before and only one German bomber was lost over the United Kingdom that day:

Oberleutnant **Johann-Heinrich Hellmers,** *Staffel Kapitaen* **Stab/KG 2**

Because the weather forecast for 23 August was not favourable, no sorties were planned for KG 2. However, the *Stabstaffel* was to carry out a reconnaissance flight and *Stoerangriffe* on the engine factory at Coventry if the weather conditions permitted. According to the weather station, it seemed possible to carry out this mission. I took off

---

[10] B3 was the code for KG 54.

from St Leger near Cambrai first, the other crews would follow at thirty minute intervals.

However, as we approached the Straits of Dover I noticed that the weather conditions were worse than forecast. We crossed the coast near Cap Gris Nez, entered cloud and flew around to the east of London. I wanted both to ascertain where I was and to get the wind strength and direction to get my bearings for Coventry. The clouds were now at 800m and we were flying just underneath them with the aircraft on auto-pilot. Whilst I was occupied with reckoning the course, the *Bordmechaniker* reported an aerodrome with bomb craters below us to the left. I could not see it from my seat on the right of the cockpit but a moment later, the airfield's anti-aircraft defences opened fire and a few seconds later, our aircraft was hit in the port engine which then caught fire. The tail was also hit.

Oblt *Johann-Heinrich Hellmers*, Stab/KG 2. (Hellmers)

Immediately, the pilot turned into clouds and to try and extinguish the fire, we side-slipped. Doing this, we lost a lot of height but we managed to put the fire out at an altitude of 150–200m. To try and reduce the plane's weight, we dropped the bombs blind in a field but the anti-aircraft fire had also affected the starboard engine, the engine speed reduced by about 100rpm and numerous instruments and the radio failed. The attempt to fly back on one engine (we had succeeded

Do 17Z coded U5+BA of Stab/KG 2 *on a training flight.* (Schlegel)

doing this a few days before) failed because we were descending at a rate of 1.5 metres per second. It was too low to bale out so the only thing to do was to force-land.

After we had stopped, we tried to set the plane on fire with incendiary bombs. Mine did not ignite and although the *Bordmechaniker* managed to put his bomb into a hole he had made in the wing, when he left the aircraft, the bomb slipped out. By then, Home Guard had hurried over and we were taken prisoner.

All were very friendly and there was an amusing event. The leader of the unit had taken away my flying suit, camera, money and cigarettes but he forgot to take my pistol. Only when I asked him what to do with it in captivity did he tell me to hand it over. Well the Sergeant standing next to us had a lot of fun – it was probably his first capture of prisoners of war! Kept under guard, I was taken to a big oak tree and whilst I was thinking about my situation, two soldiers brought me a packet of cigarettes and a mug of tea. We were then taken by bus to the airfield which had shot us down.[11]

The report which appeared in the local paper a week later was similarly amusing:

Bury Free Press and Post, 31 August 1940

Another Dornier crashed in a field of clover in an isolated parish a few miles away on Friday, apparently damaged by both British anti-aircraft guns and fighters. The four occupants, who were unhurt, climbed out and surrendered to a gamekeeper, Mr Lewis Frith, who was armed with a pitchfork and was accompanied by his two gun dogs. Mr Frith's first action was to tap the pocket of the first German he came to for his revolver which was at once handed over to him. The others handed their automatics to an Army officer who came up.

All four Germans spoke English. The Germans were equipped with little cases containing their personal belongings and from these, they produced peppermints and chocolate which they insisted in offering to their captors. Some mention was made of the war whereupon one of them exclaimed "One year September!" Another of the crew was anxious to know whether he would be allowed to write home and naturally received assurances on this point. The military then took charge. One interesting point was a little red, white and blue ring painted on one wing and bearing a date. This was a hole where repair had obviously been made to the fabric and was possibly a memento of a previous clash with British fighters.

---

[11] Believed to be Stradishall in Suffolk.

24 August saw the *Luftwaffe* increasing its efforts to annihilate Fighter Command both in the air and on the ground – the third and, for the RAF, most critical phase of the Battle of Britain had begun. The day wasn't made easier for the RAF when a series of problems with the reporting system allowed early morning German aircraft to meander over southern England with relative impunity. The new German tactic of 'rolling' one attack into another made it difficult to separate one attack from another but in the east, targets were the airfields of Hornchurch, North Weald and Manston whilst to the west, I and III/KG 51 attacked Portsmouth Harbour. The latter attack clearly illustrated the nightmare that RAF controllers were experiencing that day when the majority of the defending fighters were sent to patrol at a much lower altitude. The result was that the German formation was some 5,000ft above the Spitfires and Hurricanes and able to attack almost unmolested. Over 100 civilians were killed and well over 200 injured in addition to around fifty Royal Navy personnel. 200 bombs landed both in the Dockyard and City and the resulting fires raged for over twenty-four hours. The Germans lost one bomber to *Flak* and three fighters. The raid was a total success.

The first day of Phase Three of the Battle of Britain was in general a success for the Germans. It also saw the RAF's turret-armed Boulton Paul Defiant being badly mauled by German fighters (a similar mauling four days later resulted in the Defiant, like the *Stuka*, being withdrawn from the front line). The Germans lost eleven bombers in combat throughout the day and a number of those aircraft contained Executive Officers. *Maj* Friedrich Moericke, *Gruppen Kommandeur* of II/KG 76 was killed in the attack on Manston whilst the attack on Hornchurch by KG 53 resulted in the *Staffel Kapitaen* of 9/KG 53 of just three days, *Hptm* Heinz Loncier, being taken prisoner whilst *Maj* Kurt Ritscherle from *Stab* III/KG 53 had the misfortune of being shot down by one of the Defiants which hadn't been damaged in combat earlier in the day:

Pilot Officer Michael Young, 264 Squadron

I have rather vague memories of the action on 24 August 1940. However, I do remember flying as Number 2 to Sqn Ldr Hunter and that twenty Ju 88s were attacking Manston airfield. I remember following Philip Hunter seawards when we were attacked by Me 109s and became separated in the ensuing dogfight. Sqn Ldr Hunter failed to return from that patrol.

The next entry in my logbook was for a second patrol during which I recall finding a lone He 111 flying north towards Colchester. We used the classic Defiant attack approaching from under his port side and LAC Russell, my gunner, fired up into his belly. I don't recall any return fire and after what seemed a long time and without the German taking much avoiding action, he eventually crashed near a reservoir somewhere south of Colchester. I vaguely recall seeing a parachute.

That night, German bombers continued their attacks and were virtually unopposed. The RAF did try to intercept some of these attackers – Plt Off Bob Braham flying a Bristol Blenheim of 29 Squadron claimed to have probably destroyed a Heinkel 111 near the Humber Estuary whilst Flt Lt James Sanders flying a 615 Squadron Hurricane claimed to have destroyed a Junkers 88 and damaged a Heinkel 111. The only loss that can be matched to these three claims is *Fw* Alois Schmaderer's Heinkel 111 of 9/KG 55 which was shot down into the Channel south of Hastings (by Sanders) after attacking Harwell airfield.

During daylight on 25 August 1940, the *Luftwaffe* did not put in an appearance in strength until late in the afternoon. Simultaneously, the Junkers 88s of KG 51 attacked the airfield of Warmwell in Dorset whilst Dornier 17s of KG 76 attacked Hawkinge in Kent. The former attack was broken up by the RAF fighters, even though seven Junkers 88s managed to attack the airfield, and two bombers were shot down. The attack on Hawkinge was turned back for the loss of one Dornier 17.

That night, as the German bombers headed for British targets, RAF bombers headed for the German capital in a reprisal for the bombs that had been inadvertently dropped by the *Luftwaffe* on London the previous night. The damage caused was slight but the effect on German civilian morale was considerable. The night war was starting to escalate.

Three separate raids took place on 26 August 1940. First of all, the airfields at Biggin Hill, West Malling and Kenley were targeted by Dornier 17s of KG 3 and, it is believed, Heinkel 111s of KG 53. The RAF succeeded in preventing the German bombers from attacking their intended targets. A few hours later, the Dornier 17s of I/KG 2 took off to attack Hornchurch and III/KG 2 to attack Debden. Although Debden was bombed by a small number of Dornier 17s, the seven RAF squadrons that intercepted the formation succeeded in breaking up the attack. Six bombers were shot down and countless others damaged. Only four aircrew were killed but a further fifteen were taken prisoner, including *Maj* Martin Gutzmann, *Gruppen Kommandeur* of I/KG 2; a further seven were wounded including *Oblt* Gottfried Buchholz, *Staffel Kapitaen* of 3/KG 2. Meanwhile as this raid was returning to the Continent, to the west fifty-one Heinkel 111s of KG 55 were headed for Portsmouth Docks. Just four squadrons intercepted successfully, again preventing serious damage to the intended target and shooting down four bombers and damaging a number of others. To add insult to injury, a Heinkel 59 of *Seenotflugkommando* 2 flown by *Ofw* Herbert Eggers was shot down by Fg Off Paul Webb of 602 Squadron just before nightfall, having been engaged in picking up those bomber and fighter crews fortunate to have survived ditching – the four man crew were all killed.

The attack on Portsmouth was the last major daylight attack by *Luftflotte* 3 until the end of September 1940. Robbed of all its fighter aircraft, which had

The Do 17Z which contained Maj Gutzmann, Gr Kdr I/KG 2, *lies in a field near Eastchurch.*

moved to the Pas de Calais, its bombers concentrated on relatively less dangerous night time operations and, as a result, losses were reduced dramatically, albeit for the time being.

27 August 1940 was another one of those days punctuated by drizzle and low cloud and the occasional German incursion and loss. However, 28 August saw the start of concerted efforts by the *Luftwaffe* solely against airfields in the south east of England. The chosen targets were Eastchurch and Rochford in the morning and the massive German fighter escort inflicted serious casualties amongst the intercepting fighters especially the Defiants of 264 Squadron who lost three of their number to JG 26, with at least another four damaged; the Defiant played no further part in the Battle of Britain after this day. In the early afternoon, Dornier 17s of KG 3 again attacked Rochford, 6/KG 3 losing the only German bomber shot down as a direct result of attacks by RAF fighters on this day:

Gefreiter Willy Gailer, 6/KG 3

I joined KG 3 in June or July 1940 together with pilot Krug [*Lt* Peter Krug], *Beobachter* Reinhardt [*Gefr* Robert Reinhardt][12] and gunner Brueckmann [*Flg* Anton Brueckmann] at Schweinfurt where we learned to fly the Do 17 and we were shot down on our second or third war flight against England.

I remember we were ordered to attack an airbase – I do not know

[12] Reinhardt was wounded in action on 15 August 1940 and was replaced by *Gefr* Artur Burghardt.

Left to right Gefr *Reinhard*, Gefr *Burghardt*, Gefr *Brueckmann*. (Krug)

where exactly – and whilst flying over England in formation, we were hit by anti-aircraft fire and our aircraft lost speed and fell back. After a while, we were far behind our *Staffel* and were attacked by two Spitfires. Being the *Bordfunker*, I had to handle the upper rear machine guns so I tried to keep the attacking fighters away from us as did my comrade Brueckmann who fired the bottom rear gun. I am sure that one of the fighters was hit by our gunfire because he did not carry out further attacks against us. The other Spitfire continued to attack us and I became seriously wounded with the result that I was unable to shoot back any more. Anton Brueckmann suffered the same. I remember the pilot, *Lt* Krug, tried to escape by flying the plane at low level straight back to our base at Antwerp but he had no chance. As far as I still remember, we finally ditched in the Channel and the plane sank immediately. We were then picked up by fishermen and taken to a hospital in Margate.

Lt *Krug's Do 17 Z, June 1940.* (Krug)

Leutnant **Peter Krug,** *Staffel Fuehrer* **6/KG 3**

It was a normal take off, after briefing about the target to be attacked. When we reached the coast near Folkestone, the anti-aircraft guns began to fire but did no harm to us. Reaching the Thames Estuary short of Southend, we were hit in the port engine which began to burn. The fire was put out by the extinguisher but from then on the engine was out of action. This forced me to dive down and turn out to sea to get home but we were intercepted by fighters and shot down.

Lt *Peter Krug.* (Krug)

Squadron Leader James Leathart, 54 Squadron

I sighted twenty-four Do 17s at 16,000ft over Manston. I dived to make a head on attack on the leader but couldn't get him in my sights. Pulling up again, I found a single Do 17 going home. I gave it a quarter attack from starboard and enemy aircraft crashed into the sea off North Foreland.

Lt Krug is brought ashore at Margate.

For the bombers, the day finished there. In the late afternoon, *Freie Jagd* carried out by a number of *Jagdgeschwadern* resulted in the destruction of eight RAF fighters. This was the sort of thing that the RAF wanted to avoid – heavy losses themselves with minimal casualties inflicted on the enemy. Trouble was, exactly the same occurred the following day. Apparently using a few bombers as bait, in excess of 500 German fighters sprung a trap on the thirteen intercepting RAF squadrons and this and a later *Freie Jagd* cost the RAF nine fighters. The only German bombers lost that day were due to the inevitable accidents. However, during the night a Heinkel 111 of 3/KG 27 was shot down by a Spitfire of 92 Squadron flown by Plt Off Alan Wright and a Dornier 17 of 6/KG 2 was so badly damaged by an unidentified night fighter that it was written off on its return to France.

Gefr *Willy Gailer had the luxury of a stretcher.* (Fright)

August 1940 had indeed been a dark month for Great Britain and especially the RAF. With just two days of the month remaining and the weather forecast for those two days predicted fine conditions, it was to be expected that Fighter Command would still get no rest. With the German fighter units previously based to the west of France now established in the Pas de Calais, the German bomber crews must have felt confident as they lifted off from their airfields on the morning of 30 August 1940. The pattern of raids on that day is confused but it is believed that the first attack was by KG 1 which was briefed to attack Farnborough. The formation was broken up in a concerted attack by a number of fighter squadrons. The German unit lost five Heinkel 111s, including that flown by the *Staffel Kapitaen* of 5/KG 1, *Hptm* Rudi Baess, which was rammed by a Hurricane flown by Plt Off Edward Morris of 79 Squadron. Close on the heels of this attack was another by Dornier 17s of II/KG 76 against Biggin Hill. Immediately after lunch, more attacks materialised, one of the later attacks causing serious damage to Biggin Hill. This was carried out by the fighter-bombers of *Erprobungsgruppe* 210. However, the largest attack of the afternoon was against the Vauxhall Factory at Luton and the Handley Page Factory at Radlett:

Leutnant Ernst Fischbach, 7/KG 53

The weather that day was good. The briefing for the crew was about half an hour before take off which was scheduled for 1600 hrs. Twenty-seven He 111s took part in that raid to Radlett. I was the leader of the right *Kette* – the *Staffel Kapitaen* was *Hptm* Heinz Zorn.

After take off, all the planes met up and climbed to 9,000ft en route for Calais. Over Calais the fighters came to protect us. They did this but could not

Lt *Ernst Fischbach, July 1940.* (Fischbach)

prevent us from being attacked. The RAF fighters came relatively late when our fighters, low on fuel, had turned back for base. The bombers, now alone, tried to go on and shortly after Maidstone, the first attack was under way. About seven or eight Hurricanes came slanting up from underneath and the opposite direction, spraying machine gun bullets into the bombers. After the third attack, my starboard engine was hit and it was impossible to keep up with the formation so I tried to get out towards the North Sea (in the direction of Blackwater Estuary) but three fighters caught me again and I had to change my mind. My crew were severely injured – two had been killed and two were so badly injured that they would have been unable to

The Gruppen Kommandeur *of III/KG 53,* Maj *Friedrich Edler von Braun, inspects* Lt *Fischbach and his crew.* (Fischbach)

bale out and I couldn't leave the cockpit to help them. After belly landing, I got all out of the burning plane apart from *Gefr* Stilp.

Many of the bombers made it to the target only to get shot down on the way home:

Leutnant Wulff Roessler, 3/KG 53

We started (*Uffz* Gall, *Uffz* von Kuenheim and myself) from Vitry en Artois with our He 111 H-3 coded A1+CL and landed a short time later at Lille to change the aircraft because we had engine trouble. We shifted over to A1+IL with her *Bordmechaniker Uffz* Saam and gunner *Ogefr* Fischer.

KG 53 assembled over St Omer and picked up the fighters and headed towards the target north of London. Our position was on the right side of our *Gruppe*. Later on some British fighters appeared some 3,000ft above us and dived square into us, firing with all guns. We got one or more hits in the cooling system of our starboard engine and four minutes later had to stop the engine and feather the propellers. *Uffz* Gall was a good

Lt *Wulff Roessler (left).* (Roessler)

pilot and he easily trimmed the aircraft for single-engined flight. We overcharged the other engine and were able to hold our position in the *Gruppe*. We dropped our bombs at the same time as the others and turned for home.[13]

The *Gruppe* increased its speed to keep up with our fighters but we could not keep up with them and fell more and more behind. We could not dive to keep up with them so climbed to 14,000ft. Then an attack by fighters set the right wing on fire and killed or wounded von Kuenheim, Saam and Fischer. It was impossible for me to remove them from their seats to man their guns.

Some time later, a Bf 110 flown by *Lt* Walter Manhard with his wounded rear gunner flew under our aircraft to be protected by us, allowing him to escape from RAF fighters. I met Manhard later and he told me the full story.[14]

A few minutes later, bullets from a Hurricane destroyed our elevators and Gall and I both had to bail out...

Sergeant Henry Merchant, 'A' Flight, 1 Squadron

I was Number 2 of Red Section and upon sighting the enemy, followed my Section Leader into line astern. After attacking a Do 17 [sic] which was in company with another enemy aircraft, an Me 110 dived on me from astern. Breaking away, I shook him off and then saw ahead a single He 111. Climbing and going ahead, I attacked from the beam. On the second attack, the port engine stopped. At this moment, a Hurricane from another squadron dived from the rear of the He 111 and got in a burst. Again, by attacking from the front, I got in a long burst and a man jumped by parachute. A further two parachutists jumped after about a minute as I put in another burst. The aircraft dived and crashed in the middle of a road near a cemetery to the east of Southend.

The remains of Wulff Roessler's He 111 strewn over a Southend road. (via Cornwell)

---

[13] The Vauxhall Works were badly damaged – over fifty were killed and over 100 injured.
[14] *Lt* Manhard was from 6/ZG 26; his *Bordfunker*, *Uffz* Franz Lechmann, had been wounded by RAF fighters north of Sudbury. On 3 September 1940 and with a new *Bordfunker*, Manhard was shot down and taken prisoner.

Leutnant **Wulff Roessler**

Gall, as a pilot, had an automatic parachute and because I opened my parachute by hand, he hung above me. This was the last I saw of him until we met on a ship on the way to Canada in January 1941. Then I talked with him for ten minutes – this was the first and last time we met after the crash. Twelve minutes later I landed on the shore of the Thames, between many people in swimming costumes. Nobody said a word and I was picked up by Home Guardsmen. In silence, I was taken by lorry to a training camp. There, a friendly Scottish sergeant put me with a German fighter pilot.[15] The next evening, I was interrogated by an RAF flight lieutenant together with two other officers. I only gave my rank and name and did not answer any other questions. The investigator became more and more angry then he said "Well, you did your duty and I did mine. It was not necessary to answer my questions because I know more than you do!" He then told me all about my *Staffel* and Vitry and so on.

A few more minor attacks took place before dark. II/KG 76, for example, attacked Detling without any noticeable results before the darkness allowed those units who had not been in action during the day to set forth. Amongst others, KGr 100 launched fifteen Heinkel 111s against Liverpool and Birkenhead that night with a further two attacking Plymouth.

He 111s of 3/KGr 100 set forth on another mission. (Schick)

[15] This was *Oblt* Helmut Rau, *Staffel Kapitaen* of 3/JG 3. However, Rau had been shot down twenty-four hours later so it is believed that the two officers actually met up the next day.

The RAF had been put under terrible pressure throughout the first full day of attacks in this new phase and the intensity of the attacks in the south east had needed at least twenty-two squadrons to be committed. Of those, many were in action more than once during the day. In addition to the daylight attacks, the RAF was almost powerless to counter the attacks by night. 30 August 1940 had seen the RAF flying its largest number of sorties so far during the Battle for the loss of twenty-one aircraft in combat and nine pilots killed. The *Luftwaffe*, in their biggest effort for two weeks, lost forty aircraft.

31 August 1940 started where the previous day had left off with 'rolling' attacks taking place from first until last light. The first bombers did not appear until 0945 hrs when the Dornier 17s of II and III/KG 2 crossed the Essex coast headed for the airfields at Debden and Duxford. Other airfields were targeted throughout the day included North Weald, Eastchurch, Croydon, Biggin Hill and Hornchurch; the latter two airfields were attacked twice during the afternoon and early evening. The second attack on Hornchurch was undertaken by the Dornier 17s of I and II/KG 76. They fared better than KG 3 which had lost three Dornier 17s in the earlier attack and only one bomber was lost:

Unteroffizier Albert Bloss, 2/KG 76

On 1 September 1939, the campaign against Poland started. During that time I flew eighteen missions. From 10 May 1940, we flew thirty-eight missions against France. During my tenth mission against Great Britain, I was shot down on 31 August 1940.

Over Hornchurch, our Dornier was attacked by anti-aircraft whereby the right engine stopped and so we were forced to leave the bomber formation. *Ofw* Lang was so badly wounded in the left leg that later on it was amputated in hospital.

Later on, we were attacked by five Spitfires. One of them approached our aircraft from the back in the so-called 'dead angle' of my machine gun. Some moments later I was badly wounded in the crown of the head which gave me cerebral damage and a total paralysis except in the left arm. The pilot and *Beobachter* were not wounded.

The Do 17Z of 2/KG 76 shot down on 31 August 1940.

After the crash-landing, we were captured by British soldiers and taken to a local hospital. On arriving there, I lost consciousness for a week...

Sketches made by Fw *Harald Pfaehler depict the combat on 31 August 1940.*
(Pfaehler)

Sergeant Maurice Pocock, Blue 4, 72 Squadron

I took off from Biggin Hill at 1745 hrs as Blue 4. We climbed to 17,000ft. The Sqn Ldr led us at enemy aircraft. As I was doing rearguard, I saw one Do 215 [sic] away from the rest of the formation with starboard engine smoking, losing height slowly. I carried out a Number 1 attack. I fired 240 rounds but had to break away owing to fire from behind. I dived to 10,000ft then climbed back to the scene of the engagement and searched around for the enemy aircraft. As I could not see any after a five minute search, I returned to Biggin Hill.

It sounds as if I selected a 'lame duck' and this does not show me up in a good light! However, perhaps he was a legitimate target anyway.

As darkness fell, the RAF pilots must have been relieved that the day was over, even if they were unable to defend against the German bombers which were about to take off to bomb targets under the cover of darkness. Thirty-eight of their fighters had been shot down and eight pilots killed; a further twenty-two pilots were wounded whilst the *Luftwaffe* had lost about thirty-eight aircraft. A change in *Luftwaffe* tactics now meant that it concentrated on one part of the United Kingdom which included Fighter Command airfields and aircraft production. It used rolling attacks escorted by a considerable and aggressive fighter force. RAF losses were increasing and they could not continue to replace losses inflicted by German fighters over the past two days if this trend continued. The Germans would continue to adopt the current tactics but only for a week after which fortunes were destined to change for both sides.

Sgt Maurice Pocock in belligerent mood.
(Lamberton)

3
The Beginning of the End – September 1940

September 1940 started exactly where August left off with the first bombers arriving over Kent mid-morning making for Biggin Hill, Detling and Eastchurch airfields and London Docks (the Docks apparently being retaliation for the RAF attacks on Berlin). After lunch, it was Biggin Hill again as well as Kenley and Gravesend. German losses were light – only one bomber was shot down during the whole day, thanks mainly to the massive German fighter escort. This loss was a Dornier 17 of 9/KG 76 in whose crew was *Lt* Wilhelm Illg. Two weeks before on 18 August 1940, *Ofw* Illg had been a *Beobachter* in one of the Dornier 17s of 9/KG 76 briefed to carry out the low level attack on Kenley. His pilot, *Oblt* Hermann Magin had been mortally wounded and Illg had flown the damaged bomber back to France. This time, he and two of the crew of four were captured; Illg was later to receive the *Ritterkreuz* for his bravery on 18 August.

Again the day had been a bad one for the RAF, losing twelve aircraft in combat. Four of these came from 85 Squadron with Sgt (soon to be Plt Off) Geoffrey Allard being the pilot responsible for shooting down *Lt* Illg's bomber. The Operations Record Book entry for the afternoon of 1 September shows how the Squadron was suffering:

F540 Operations Record Book – 85 Squadron

Squadron again airborne at 1350 hrs to intercept enemy formation approaching Tunbridge Wells/Kenley area. At about 1355 hrs, about 150–200 aircraft (Do 17, Me 109 and Me 110) were sighted near Biggin Hill at 15,000ft. When sighted, the Squadron was still about 5,000ft lower and while climbing, were attacked continuously by 109s and 110s. Sgt Allard attacked a straggling Do 17 whose rear gunner baled out and whose pilot attempted a forced landing near the railway line at Lydd. Allard's oil pressure dropped and so he switched off and landed at Lympne but while the aircraft was being serviced, the airfield was bombed and his aircraft hit. Plt Off English carried out two quarter attacks on a Do 17 [sic] stopping its starboard engine; the enemy aircraft landed between Ham Street and Hythe and two of the crew were seen to emerge.[1] Sgt Evans attacked and destroyed an Me 109 with a seven second burst and an Me 110 with a five second burst but was unable to identify location of crashes. Sgt Howes attacked and shot down a Do 17 just south of Tunbridge Wells, two crew members baling out. He also damaged an Me 109. Fg Off Gowers was hit by a cannon shell and baled out with severe burns on hands and wounds in hands and foot; his Hurricane crashed at Oxted. Sgt Booth's aircraft was hit by cannon shells; he baled out near Purley and his aircraft crashed at Sanderstead. His parachute did not open properly and he suffered a broken back, leg and arm. Fg Off Woods-Scawen was posted missing and his body was found near Kenley on 6 September – his parachute unopened. Sgt Ellis was also killed in this fight. Six Hurricanes – all that remained of the Squadron – landed at Croydon between 1430 hrs and 1500 hrs and Plt Off Lewis had to land wheels up.

After a relatively quiet night for the German bombers, the attacks on 2 September 1940 followed a similar pattern to the previous day but this time started much earlier in the morning and lasted into the early evening. Similar targets were chosen and, yet again, only one German bomber was shot down by RAF fighters although two more Dornier 17s from the same unit, 9/KG 3, were written off on their return to France. The pattern looked to be the same for 3 September but the early morning attack by KG 2 on North Weald turned out to be the only major one of the day. The majority of German losses were fighters and, yet again, just one Dornier 17 (from 5/KG 2) was lost. That night the nocturnal bombers were again roaming all over the United Kingdom which forced one Hurricane squadron to take action:

87 Squadron Diary Entry – 3 September 1940

It was decided that 87 Squadron would start night flying again so 'B' Flight moved off to Bibury. The weather was about as good as possible for night flying and on the first night, Plt Off Beamont engaged an enemy aircraft south east of Bristol. He hit it but could not see the results.

No damage was reported to any German aircraft. For the moment, the German bombers were still relatively safe.

4 September saw no let up in the German bomber offensive. The first raid (by Dornier 17s of KG 76 against the airfields of Rochford, Eastchurch and Lympne) had no perceivable results but it is believed that this raid also hit the Shorts Aircraft Factory at Rochester, causing minor damage to the production

[1] This was in fact a Messerschmitt 110 of 13/LG1- *Ofw* Rudolf Kobert and *Fw* Werner Meinig were both captured.

line. However, the most noteworthy attack was by *Erprobungsgruppe* 210 against the airfield at Brooklands near Weybridge, the airfield being the home of the Vickers Aircraft factory. The attack was in two phases – as a larger formation headed towards targets in Kent, the fighter-bombers headed towards their target, reaching it for the loss of just one aircraft (that flown by its new *Gruppen Kommandeur Hptm* Hans von Boltenstern). They succeeded in stopping production for a number of days and causing the deaths of eighty-eight workers with countless others injured. This attack was particularly fortuitous for the *Luftwaffe* as Hitler was now becoming increasingly infuriated by the RAF's bombing attacks on the German homeland, particularly Berlin which had been bombed following the *Luftwaffe*'s bombing of London on the night of 24/25 August. Hitler now declared that the time for reprisals had come and this heralded the start of the *Luftwaffe*'s major nocturnal attacks against London – the London Blitz was about to start.

That night saw an increase in German night attacks and, at last, RAF night fighters started to meet with success:

A Ju 88 A of 4/KG 51 taxies out to bomb a British target. (Ciuraj)

A He 111 lifts off to bomb Britain.

Oberleutnant **Peter Biebrach,** *Gruppen Technischer Offizier, Stab* **I/KG 1**

By August 1940, we had moved forward to the airfield at Montdidier for attacks against targets in England, partly large scale day raids but mostly night raids by individual aircraft. Targets were chosen in a somewhat unsystematic manner or so it seemed. One night we might attack an industrial complex such as the Rolls Royce Works, another day an airfield or a Navy installation might be picked.

On 4 September, a report came in from Headquarters that two or three warships, thought to be destroyers, had pulled into Tilbury Docks and that we had to attack the Docks that night. Our crew was selected and in the usual pre-flight briefings we heard that the target might be protected by balloons in addition to anti-aircraft batteries. The weather was said to be fair with light cloud cover over the target area and with a light wind. It seemed logical that any defence would be aimed towards the south therefore it was decided to fly past the target and attack on the way back, flying as low as possible. This was easier said than done as there was no moon to help us in seeing what was ahead of the aircraft. Also, it was decided to fly on a course which would take us mid-way between Tilbury and the City of London (I would have preferred to have flown further east). We were to fly at 6,000m and night fighters were not expected. This was my fortieth war flight and I had flown by night against England many times before and hadn't once been opposed by night fighters, *Flak* or been picked up by searchlights.

We were scheduled to be over the target at 0100 hrs but, just before take off, *Ofw* Stockert (the upper gunner) reported that his gun would not move and was jammed. The *Gruppen Kommandeur* [*Maj* Ludwig Maier] and I thought about this for a moment and then decided that as it was unlikely that we would need the gun, we would continue. As will be seen, we were to regret this decision.

Contrary to our weather reports, the sky was cloudless over England, offering us no protection in case of trouble. Also, the westerly wind seemed to be somewhat stronger that anticipated. We tried to correct our course but not in time to avoid the defences around London. Our aircraft, in particular the underside of the fuselage and wings, had been painted with a water-based paint so as to offer no reflection. However, our aircraft were parked outside away from the airfield and prior to take off passed over tall patches of weeds and I assume that on that evening, some of this paint had been washed or worn away. Therefore, much to our surprise, we were suddenly picked up by two or three searchlights and in seconds were firmly held by many others which made it almost impossible to see anything in the cockpit. Seconds later, we were the target of a great number of anti-aircraft guns with well aimed salvoes. We could smell the gunpowder from the exploding shells and the noise was incredible. However, we received no direct hits and there was no vital damage to the aircraft, as far as we could determine.

Black distemper applied to both a He 111 and its bomb load.
(Hoehler)

After a few minutes, the guns fell silent which was a relief to us but should have alerted us to some other trouble since we were still illuminated. A minute or so later, *Ofw* Stockert called that he could see something approaching. I reacted by taking the aircraft into a sharp right-hand turn. Almost simultaneously, I saw a great number of tracers fly past my port side followed by the attacking aircraft which I identified as a Blenheim. This surprised us as the Blenheim was thought to be slower than the Heinkel 111 and I surmised that he must have attacked from a higher altitude and it followed that he would not be able to repeat the attack as he was now below us. We therefore went back on course and continued our mission. However, without warning we were attacked again – the oxygen bottles exploded, leaving me temporarily unconscious due to the lack of oxygen. The port engine had partly sheared off and was spewing oil and wreckage – I managed to feather the propeller before the engine seized with a thud. Again, I made a sharp turn to starboard and pushed the nose down so as to escape the fighter...

Pilot Officer Michael Herrick, 25 Squadron

At about 0020 hrs, I took off from Martlesham to patrol a patrol line. I received a vector and then the wireless became unserviceable. After about ten minutes, I sighted an enemy aircraft ahead in searchlights but was unable to close and it drew away out of sight. Then at about 500ft above me, I sighted an enemy aircraft in a searchlight and attacked after five minutes. I opened fire at about 300 to 400 yards with a five second burst. Then the enemy aircraft disappeared. Immediately afterwards, another enemy aircraft was illuminated and after chasing for about ten minutes, I got within range and opened fire at about 400 yards. I then fired several short bursts with the range decreasing and obtained a good defection shot. The enemy aircraft seemed to halt and wave in the air and I overshot as I had used all my remaining ammunition. The searchlights turned on me and I was unable to see any more. As I overtook enemy aircraft, I noticed that it was falling to pieces and both engines were smoking badly. My rear gunner, Sgt Pugh, fired in both actions.

Oberleutnant Peter Biebrach

...We came out of the range of the searchlights but had lost some 2,000m altitude. The starboard engine was starting to overheat and was idling so as to give us enough electricity to light the instrument panel and give power for the landing lights. *Maj* Maier had gone to the rear of the aircraft and had established that both men there [*Ofw* Erwin Stockert and *Uffz* Horst Bendig] were dead and that there was considerable damage. However, the aircraft responded to all controls.

A large white 'stream' was seen further ahead and both the *Gruppen Kommandeur* and the *Beobachter* [*Oblt* Job-Wilhelm Graf von Rittberg] were of the opinion that this was the River Thames. I knew that this was impossible as we were still heading north-east and had passed the Thames a long time ago. I advised that we should leave the aircraft and had a brief argument over this whilst still losing altitude. When the decision to bale out was reached, Graf von Rittberg could not find his parachute until I remembered that the *Gruppen Kommandeur* had been sitting on it. With the parachute then in place, the starboard exit door was jettisoned and Graf von Rittberg flung himself out followed by *Maj* Maier. They had approximately 1,400m to drop. In the meantime, I had opened the door above my seat and climbed onto my seat squatting there ready to get out whilst holding the aircraft level. I left at an altitude of approximately 400m, pushed myself off the top of the fuselage (the aircraft was climbing suddenly and slowing accordingly) and I fell counting to three rather fast, pulled the rip cord and the parachute opened instantly. A few seconds later, I found myself on the ground in the middle of a fairly large clearing. It was shortly after 0130 hrs on 5 September 1940. I did not know it then but the war for me was over and it would be another six years and two months before I saw Germany again.

At about 0600 hrs, I attempted to orientate myself and to find a way out of the forest. As I had a severely sprained ankle and a sore back, this was a difficult task at first. I managed to find a country road and was unsuccessful at stopping a man on his bike and I arrived after about an hour in a little village and I tried to find some signs pointing to places

The fuselage of Peter Biebrach's He 111. (via Cornwell)

that I might know. A blacksmith probably mistook me for a British pilot and asked me into his house and his equally friendly wife served me a tremendous and most welcome English breakfast – I have sported her recipe ever since! I was then found standing in the yard by two policemen who had been alerted by the man on the bike. Both sported infantry guns with the bayonets in place. They carried out a perfect pincer movement towards me and I could not help but laugh. I was then placed in the rear of their little Austin and we drove off. First to the families of the policemen where I was given two more breakfasts, a bandage for my foot and new socks. Then we drove off to Ipswich where I was handed over to Police Headquarters. Shortly before getting to the town, one of the policemen remembered that they should have searched me so I was told to get out and their search produced my fully loaded Walther automatic. Having never seen one before, they handed it back to me so that I could unload it for them. I obliged.

For the next two days of September 1940, destined to be the last two days of this phase of the Battle of Britain, Fighter Command was again put under extreme pressure with a series of 'rolling' attacks against airfields. However, on the night of 5 September, the new die was cast when *Luftflotte* 2 launched its first major night attack against London, using bombers from four different *Geschwadern*. Then, on 7 September 1940, German tactics changed again.

Pressure from Hitler, and a realisation that all-out attacks on RAF fighter airfields had not destroyed the RAF, resulted in the *Luftwaffe* throwing its might against the British capital. It was hoped that the British will to fight, on seeing London being pounded day and night by German bombs, would falter and the RAF would be forced to commit all of its remaining fighters in defence of the Nation's capital; German fighters would then destroy the remaining Spitfires and Hurricanes. History has now shown that this was yet another German misjudgement.

There was scarce German air activity until about 1600 hrs on 7 September when radar screens detected in the region of 1,000 bombers and fighters spread between altitudes of 14,000ft and 23,000ft. By 1630 hrs, more than twenty RAF fighter squadrons were either airborne or at readiness and then thrown against the attackers. The target soon became clear when the German bombers droned onwards towards London, dropping their bombs on London's Dockland and setting much of it ablaze. The attack had lasted just under an hour and the RAF succeeded in shooting down forty-one German aircraft. Just over half of those lost were escorting fighters which had enabled the bombers to reach their target. The RAF lost twenty-two fighters but only ten pilots lost their lives.

Night came early to London on 7 September, brought about by the palls of smoke drifting from its Dockland. The *Luftwaffe* bombers came again that night on what now has been called the official first night of the Blitz and more civilian lives were lost. However, the start of the final phase of the Battle of Britain, with the *Luftwaffe* bombing commercial and civilian targets in addition to military ones, gave Fighter Command the break they needed. It is now thought that Fighter Command could not have sustained the pressure and losses experienced during the week prior to 7 September 1940 and if that phase had not changed, the outcome of the Battle of Britain could have been very different. Relieved Fighter Command's pilots might well have been, but the Battle of Britain was destined to continue for another fifty-four days.

The German bombers came again on 8 September when II and III/KG 2 headed for two separate targets in London. Two II/KG 2 Dornier 17s from the same *Kette* were simultaneously shot down by anti-aircraft fire whilst another exploded when attacked by a Hurricane of 46 Squadron. A III/KG 2 aircraft returned damaged after apparently colliding with an unidentified British fighter. That night, London received yet another pounding – it was just the second in what would transpire to be fifty-seven consecutive nights of pounding by the *Luftwaffe*.

9 September again saw the *Luftwaffe* making another major attack on London but not until the early evening. This was a relief for Plt Offs George Forrester and Jim Humphreys of 605 Squadron. They had spent the night of 8 September in London with their 'B' Flight Commander, Flt Lt Archie McKellar, and the two were glad of the rest, not going into action that day until the Germans made their appearance:

Pilot Officer Jim Humphreys, 'B' Flight, 605 Squadron

The Squadron was ordered off at about 1700 hrs and after some fifteen minutes, 'B' Flight was detached and vectored onto this raid. We made contact at about 1725 hrs. There were some twenty to twenty-five He 111s with Me 109s as close and high escort. Our vector placed us awkwardly at the rear of the formation and slightly below and it seemed that we were climbing for ages to get into the attacking position. All this was complicated by the odd peck from the close escorts.

As the high escorts were starting to show a little too much interest, I moved Green Section [Humphreys, Plt Off Cyril Passy and Plt Off Edward Watson] outwards, drawing them with us. Blue Section [Flt Lt Archie McKellar, Sgt Jan Budzinski and Plt Off George Forrester] then managed to attack, breaking up the bomber formation, and I turned Green Section in to pick off any of the scattered Heinkels. At this point, we were bounced by the Me 110s which I had not seen. Probably they were on free range.

My aircraft was hit three or four times, one being a 20mm high explosive right beside the throttle quadrant. I went down in an aileron turn for 2,000ft to 3,000ft and took stock. There was a sizeable hole in the cockpit wall, the throttle quadrant was gone, the cockpit was full of smoke and petrol fumes and I was feeling mighty sick. It seemed that she was about to burn so I baled out. This would be about 12,000ft.

I did not want to stay in that area so I did a free fall down to cloud level (about 3,000ft) and opened my 'chute. My hand was a mess – blood, flesh, bone and glove all mixed up together – so for the rest of the descent, I was hanging grimly onto the pressure point.

I came out of cloud over a Canadian Army camp at Bordon and drifted across it with the breeze. The natives were most unfriendly and treated me as a one-man invasion force. One feels so helpless listening to stuff going past from a Lewis gun! I was lucky – six holes in the canopy, one rigging line cut and one through the left breast pocket of my tunic which left a weal on my side. Come to think of it, I was lucky that day.

I landed just outside the camp in a copse just beside a railway line, was picked up by the Canadians and, having been relieved of my buttons, maps, flying boots, etc, I was taken into Aldershot. There I was put in the Cambridge Military Hospital and remained there for about four weeks.

Although Jim Humphreys thought he was a victim of the German escort, crew from one of the German bombers that 605 Squadron was attacking thought differently only then to be confronted by another one of the 605 Squadron pilots who had been 'on the town' the night before:

Oberfeldwebel Oskar Broderix, *Stab* III/KG 53

Ofw *Oskar Broderix (right).* (Broderix)

On the afternoon of 9 September 1940, about thirty aircraft from III/KG 53 took off from Lille–Roubaix to bomb the Queen Elizabeth Docks in London. I was flying in the lead aircraft of the *Stabskette* instead of *Hptm* Heinz Zorn, *Staffel Kapitaen* of 7/KG 53. Another aircraft in the *Kette* was flown by *Oblt* Barth. This was my fiftieth war flight – I didn't think it would be any different to the others so I had brought my Leica camera to photograph London.

My *Beobachter* was different for this trip – usually it was *Oberst* Erich Stahl, the *Geschwader Kommodore*, but today it was my old *Beobachter Oblt* Kurt Meinecke. *Fw* Ernst Wendorff and *Fw* Wilhelm Wenninger had flown with me many times before but for *Fw* Willi Doering, this was his first trip.

In front of the He 111 H-2 they were flying in on 9 September 1940 are, left to right, Fw *Ernst Wendorff,* Fw *Willi Wenninger,* Oblt *Kurt Meinecke and* Ofw *Oskar Broderix.* (Broderix)

We flew at an altitude of 3,000m and waited for our escort. Then all of us flew towards London. Soon after crossing the coast, the RAF fighters attacked us and I saw many aircraft going down in flames. I cannot remember whether we were to do two passes or one over the target but we did drop some bombs and flew on west.

We were then attacked by Hurricanes which seemed to pick on the *Stabskette*. I heard Ernst Wendorff shout with joy – he had just shot down a Hurricane and we saw it go down.[2] Then another Hurricane attacked us. I heard Willi Wenninger say over the intercom "I've got him!" and then there was a crash and the controls went slack. The burning Hurricane had rammed us! I looked back and saw that the tail had been torn away and that the Heinkel was starting to break up. I remember pushing *Oblt* Meinecke out of the cockpit and then lost

---

[2] Believed to be the Hurricane flown by Plt Off Jim Humphreys.

A He 111 drops its deadly cargo.

consciousness. I awoke swinging on my parachute. I landed in a field and was captured quickly by soldiers who were brought by two girls. Later on I was taken to where my aircraft had crashed – all that I saw was a pall of oily black smoke.

Three Germans were killed in the crash just south of Alton in Hampshire; Plt Off George Forrester was killed when his Hurricane crashed just to the north of the town. It is believed that he had been mortally wounded or killed and it is conjecture as to whether he deliberately rammed the German bomber or not.

10 September saw a dramatic reduction in German air operations, bad weather being the reason for this. However, two German bombers did fall victim to Fighter Command aircraft in the evening. That night saw London, as well as Berlin and other targets in Germany, being bombed, the German bombers faring better than the RAF who lost two bombers in an attack on Bremen. Similar damage was inflicted on both capital cities.

The bad weather was still hanging around much of the United Kingdom the following day and it was not until mid-afternoon that a raid of "300+" was plotted heading towards London:

Armstrong Whitworth Whitley serial T4134 of 58 Sqn lies in the sea off Schleswig–Holstein after being shot down by flak attacking Bremen on the night of 10/11 September 1940.

Gefreiter **Wilhelm Zimmer,** *Stab* **II/KG 26**

Gefr Wilhelm Zimmer keeping a look out for trouble.
(Zimmer)

On 11 September 1940, we had been scheduled a day of rest. We were sitting in the canteen having our meal and a few beers looking forward to the rest. Then the warning came and we rushed to our accommodation to get parachutes, map cases and flying suits and then ran to our briefing. Our *Gruppen Kommandeur, Maj* Eckhard Christian announced the target as London and the flying formation.

At first we assembled over Belgium and Holland at an altitude of 5,000m and then the formation crossed the coast in the direction of London – it was then that we had a slight mishap. Because we were a crew of five and the *Kommandeurbesatzung*, there was additional oxygen for *Maj* Christian. It turned out that this had not been filled up so the *Major* and I had to share the same oxygen point!

We flew on through the *Flak* barrage. The weather was magnificent – above us a cloudless sky and at about 3,000m below us there were only a few drifting clouds. I think it was about 1600 hrs when London lay before us.

Now I heard someone yelling on the radio "Enemy fighters attacking behind us!" – this report came from our *Bordfunker* [*Ofw* Ziermann]. These fighters were Spitfires. I had already lowered my *Lotfe* bombsight and had in my sights our target – the docks along the River Thames. I leaned back a bit, looked up and saw that our fighters were involved in dogfights with British fighters about 1,000–2,000m above us. Now we were without fighter escort.

Then we heard a groaning – it was the *Bordmechaniker* [*Fw* Richard Herrmann] who had been wounded in the thigh by four bullets. The pilot [*Fw* Krothe] shouted "Drop the bombs – I cannot keep the plane under control as the engine is damaged!" Only now I noticed that I had been slightly wounded – grazes caused by splinters of perspex.

The pilot jettisoned the bombs which fell on the suburbs. The engine was switched off and we flew on with the remaining engine running fine. The British fighters flew attack after attack. The aircraft on our right flown by *Oblt* Gustav-Otto Bertram went into a spin and dropped away. All I could say was "Bertram is shot down." *Maj* Christian and I changed places. I went to the rear of the plane and took the *Bordmechaniker*'s position – when I wanted to dress his wounds, he refused and said that he had to fend off attacks.

Well, this afternoon, the RAF used really good tactics and we were not expecting that. The attacks were carried out in three waves – one from below, then one attack came horizontally and the third one involved our fighters high above us. We defended ourselves to the last cartridge – I was able to fend off some attacks from below. What happened next will always be a mystery to me. We had exhausted all our ammunition and were at the enemy's mercy. When our adversary noticed that we did not defend ourselves any more, he flew over our aircraft, wobbled his wings and dived away. After that there were no more attacks.

With our *Kette*, we curved around over London. In the place of *Oblt* Bertram, *Oblt* Ernst Haller, *Staffel Kapitaen* of 4/KG 26, now flew. My best friend *Gefr* Rudi Endrich was a member of the Bertram crew and on this day he was shot down a second time. The first time he was shot down over Narvik in Norway on 22 May 1940 but was released from captivity when the British troops retreated. I am happy to say that the Bertram crew were taken prisoner and survived.[3]

In fear and trembling, we crossed the Channel wondering how long we could stay in the air. It all went quite well until we approached our base at Gilze–Rijen in Holland. The undercarriage was lowered – it was a joy to see that it had worked and from my place in the cockpit, I checked if it was locked. I said "Everything all right!" but the last shock was to come. *Fw* Krothe came in to land and bumping and crashing, the plane turned round and round – all tyres had been shot to pieces.

Nobody had been wounded except the *Bordmechaniker* – immediately after our landing, he was transported to a hospital in Breda. Everybody was happy that we had come home safely but I still regard 11 September 1940 as a bitter defeat and a pointless waste of lives and material.

Gefr *Rudi Endrich, POW on 11 September 1940.* (Zimmer)

Despite a heavy fighter escort, the Heinkel 111s of KG 1 and especially KG 26 suffered heavy losses. KG 1 lost three bombers over England with a further two returning damaged whilst KG 26 lost seven with a further ten returning with varying degrees of damage. The majority of the losses were suffered by I/KG 26. From the *Stabskette*, one aircraft was shot down and the other two damaged whilst 1/KG 26 lost two aircraft and two damaged out of six flying that day. One 1 *Staffel* pilot, *Fw* Wilhelm Jabusch, even baled out over London and was captured, leaving his un-named *Beobachter* to fly the

Fg Off *Brian van Mentz (centre) of 222 Sqn who was credited with shooting down* Gefr *Endrich and his crew (with Sqn Ldr R C Love, Fg Off G G A Davies, Plt Off J M V Carpenter and Plt Off C Stewart).*

plane home, wrecking it in the ensuing crash-landing near Dieppe. The *Staffel Kapitaen* of 1/KG 26 would not have been impressed by this but as he too was shot down, he was not to know this:

---

[3] Three of the crew were captured; *Lt* Ferdinand Cramer, the fourth crew member, was killed.

Hauptmann Wolfgang Kuenstler, *Staffel Kapitaen* 1/KG 26

Our *Gruppe* had been at Courtrai in Belgium since 1 September 1940. On 11 September, we were briefed to attack Woolwich Arsenal. My *Gruppen Kommandeur Maj* Hermann Busch together with his *Stabskette* took command of my *Staffel* because we only had six aircraft ready for action on this day. We took off at about 1430 hrs Central European Time and had to climb and turn to meet our escort, Bf 110s of II/ZG 26. However, they were soon engaged in dogfights as soon as we crossed the coast so we had to go on by ourselves. At about 1630–1645 hrs, we were attacked by five Hurricanes coming from the front right. My *Kette* was attacked twice and after the second attack, my port engine seized and the other one caught fire. That did it! We turned away out of formation and after another attack from behind, we made an emergency landing south of Sevenoaks. Two of my crew had been killed but we succeeded in blowing the plane up with an incendiary bomb just as the good old Home Guard arrived!

Reichsmarschall *Goering visits Courtrai, 10 September 1940 – standing to his right is* Hptm *Wolfgang Kuenstler.* (Kuenstler)

The next three days were quieter, poor weather again being the reason. However, German bombers did continue to attack with relative impunity by night although losses were starting to occur, two of them indirectly as a result of the weather:

Uffz *Alwin Machalett (POW 15 August 1940)* and Uffz *Erich Schmidt (POW with* Hptm *Kuenstler, 10 September 1940)*. (Machalett)

Oberleutnant Harry Wappler, 8/KG 27

I became a prisoner of war in the early hours of Friday 13 September 1940 between 0200 hrs and 0300 hrs. My plane hit part of a barrage balloon at Newport, South Wales.

The flight above ground was about 1,200ft. Very low I know but it was very bad weather and I was eager to know whether my last two 50

The remains of Harry Wappler's He 111 in a Newport street. (via Cornwell)

kilogram bombs were on target that night. It all then happened very quickly. The cockpit disintegrated and the same second I found myself out of the plane, feeling a blow to my right arm. I never flew with the safety belt done up and this must have saved me. Before falling unconscious, probably because my right arm had been broken in three places, I managed to open my parachute. I then suffered a blackout until about 1000 hrs the next morning when I awoke in the Royal Monmouthshire Hospital in Newport. The other three members of my crew were killed.[4]

RAF night fighters were also continuing to improve their effectiveness. Plt Off Michael Herrick of 25 Squadron had already shot down one Heinkel 111 at night and on the night of the 13/14 September 1940 would repeat this feat for which he was later awarded the Distinguished Flying Cross. At 0025 hrs on 14 September, he and his gunner Plt Off Archibald Brown took off from Martlesham Heath for a patrol over London. Over an hour later, he spotted a Heinkel 111 held in the beams of ten searchlights:

Oberleutnant **Hermann Kell, Staffel Fuehrer 3/KG 4**

Officers of 3/KG 4. Front (l to r): Hptm *Karl-Gerd Roth* (St Kap), Lt *Hoehne,* Oblt *Hermann Kell,* Oblt *Klaus Born. Back:* Oblt *Fritz Bredemeier,* Lt *Hans Kalcher,* Lt *Helmut Furcht.* (Koch)

By September 1940, we were stationed at Soesterberg in Holland. On the afternoon of 13 September, we were ordered to attack London during the night. By late afternoon, the weather had become very bad and it became obvious that a number of the crews didn't have the experience to handle this weather at night.

IX *Fliegerkorps* altered the order. Only one plane was to fly a nuisance mission that night. Target: Victoria Railway Station in London. I volunteered. The weather at take off was rain and wind with cloud at 100m. I decided to climb above the cloud where I encountered turbulence and lightning like I had never encountered before. At 5,000m I pierced the cloud ceiling – it was a wonderful moonlit night with no clouds. Ahead I saw the mouth of the

---

[4] Harry Wappler's later claim to fame is that he and *Lt* Heinz Schnabel, a Messerschmitt 109 pilot from 1/JG 3, managed to escape and stole an RAF training aircraft. They succeeded in getting from Carlisle to Norfolk before running out of fuel and were soon recaptured.

Thames – my interim target. I also noticed that the heavy rain had washed off the night camouflage paint of my He 111 – the 'Lady' was shining like a waxed apple!

When I reached the Thames Estuary, I was surprised how fast the searchlights caught me in their beams. I put it down to the 'apple skin' of my He 111. It was easy to get rid of the searchlights but it was apparently equally easy for them to catch me again as soon as I was flying straight and level. The appearance of my flight to London must have resembled the tracks of a rabbit pursued by a dog. At that time, we did not know that the era of radar had begun!

Over London, I could clearly see the railway tracks leading to Victoria Station. On the approach, I stopped the evasive movements, the bomb bay was opened and the *Beobachter Fw* Walter Hobe directed me to the target; even then we were held by many searchlights. I hoped that no night fighter would be in position until I had finished but I did not know that we already had a bug on our tail despite our efforts at evading.

Suddenly, a closely packed, never ending stream of tracer bullets came from the rear and engulfed the cockpit on both sides. There was no doubt that we had received many hits. The bombs were jettisoned and I turned the plane on its port wing tip. When we were level again, I noticed that the temperature in the port engine was rising so I shut it down to give us a chance of getting back to the Continent on one engine. This idea was short-lived as the port engine then burst into flames.

I informed the crew of my intention to glide northwards and to try to reach open country to bale out. I received no answer from the rear. *Fw* Hobe went back with a torch to tell them but returned with the report that *Uffz* Hermann Toepfer (*Bordmechaniker*) and the *Bordfunker Ogefr* Werner Mueller Wernscheidt, both fine men, were dead.

We glided, burning, from 6,000m to 2,000m with *Fw* Hobe standing beside me at the ready. At 2,000m I assumed I was over open fields, trimmed the plane for the last time, we shook hands and left the plane through the emergency exit above the pilot's head. We both landed separately in open fields. We met again in the cells at Chelmsford. For both of us the experience of six and a half years behind barbed wire had begun.

What is now regarded as the climax of the Battle of Britain took place on Sunday

He 111s of I/KG 4 taxi out on a daylight mission; a member of the crew sits in the emergency escape hatch above the pilot's head. (Koch)

15 September 1940 and what happened that day has been related in many books and journals. In an attempt to ensure that the planned invasion of Great Britain could take place, the *Luftwaffe* threw its might against London, the first attack manifesting itself at 1100 hrs when fighter bombers of II/LG 2 attacked the capital for the first but not last time. Twenty minutes later, Dornier 17s of II and III/KG 76 appeared over London's suburbs:

Feldwebel Rolf Heitsch, 8/KG 76

The attack height was about 6,000m, our target a factory to the east of London, close to the Thames.[5] On the return flight as the right-hand *Kettenhund*, I was the aircraft the enemy would target. Whilst in a left hand turn, we found ourselves at the rear of the formation and it was then that the fighters attacked.[6] As the slowest Do 17, they attacked us from behind. Trying to take evasive action by flying up and down, they hit us with three bursts with the result that we only had 4/5ths power from the engines. The right engine was totally destroyed and the left engine was just idling. We managed to get between two cumulus clouds and had to force-land in a field which sloped uphill and was occupied by cows at their midday rest. When the plane came to a halt, we could not get out because the exits had been so badly damaged by gunfire.

Because there was a strong north-westerly wind, our escort had turned back for home early so we were alone over the target. We had already delayed take off by half an hour but this was not passed to the escort so we were attacked and easily shot down.

A few minutes after we had crash-landed, the Home Guard turned up and took us prisoner. My wounded crew were taken away by car and I was taken away to a police station. I was destined to be a prisoner of war until 12 May 1948.

Whilst the RAF Spitfires had gone after the fighters, the bombers were initially attacked by Hurricanes which succeeded in splitting up the formation. Shortly afterwards, the Duxford Wing, consisting of a further five fighter squadrons, joined the attack on the helpless bombers and even though KG 76 reached London, the damage they inflicted was slight and then German casualties began to rise as their Dornier 17s tried to flee for France. KG 76 lost six bombers and a further two badly damaged; the cost in human terms was twelve killed, ten prisoners of war and three wounded.

The RAF fighters landed and rearmed and were ready for the next

---

[5] It is believed that the intended target was actually the railway lines at Latchmere Junction.
[6] Eventual destruction of *Fw* Heitsch's Dornier 17 was credited to Fg Off John Dundas and Plt Off Eugene 'Red' Tobin of 609 Squadron.

A wounded crewman is taken away from Fw *Heitsch's Dornier 17.* (via Cornwell)

The same Dornier being dismantled prior to its final journey to the scrap heap. (via Cornwell)

The pilots responsible for the Dornier's demise – Fg Off John Dundas (left)...

onslaught which was this time by Dornier 17s of II and III/KG 2 and II/KG 3 and Heinkel 111s of I and II/KG 53 and I and II/KG 26. The total force of 114 bombers flew in three parallel columns three miles apart and together with its substantial escort, the whole formation stretched for some thirty miles. The targets this time were the Royal Victoria, West India and Surrey Commercial Docks in eastern London.

...and Plt Off 'Red' Tobin (right seen with Plt Off Keith Ogilvie who also claimed a Do 17 on 15 September 1940).

The RAF fighters threw themselves at the German formation and one of the greatest air battles ever seen took place over much of Kent, London and its suburbs, East Sussex and parts of Essex. However, London was spared serious damage because of the weather for when the German bombers arrived over London, they found their targets obscured by cloud. Unable to find their primary targets, their bombs were dropped on the south-eastern outskirts of the capital as they turned for home, all the time being attacked mercilessly by Spitfires and Hurricanes.

The German bombers suffered badly. KG 2 lost eight Dornier 17s and a further seven returned with varying degrees of damage; nineteen aircrew were killed, nine taken prisoner and ten wounded. KG 3 fared a little better – six aircraft destroyed and four damaged with fifteen of its II *Gruppe* aircrew killed, ten prisoners of war and four wounded. The Heinkel 111s did not suffer as badly as the Dornier 17s – KG 26 lost just one of its bombers with its crew of four being taken prisoner; a further three of its aircraft were damaged and just two crew members were wounded. KG 53 lost six aircraft with another two damaged; twelve aircrew were killed, eighteen taken prisoner (including *Maj* Max Gruber, the *Gruppen Kommandeur* of II/KG 53 and most senior German officer lost that day) and four wounded.

As this attack disappeared off the radar screens, twenty-six unescorted Heinkel 111s of I and III/KG 55 attacked Royal Navy installations at Portland and then, two hours later, *Erprobungsgruppe* 210 attacked the Supermarine Factory at Southampton. Both raids were ineffective and Plt Off Arthur Watson of 152 Squadron shot down a 9/KG 55 Heinkel 111 resulting in the deaths of three of its crew with the fourth being taken prisoner. Any further daylight attacks were cancelled because of the deteriorating weather conditions and it was again left to the German bombers to continue the onslaught against London under the cover of darkness.

The *Luftwaffe* had flown over 1,000 sorties on what is now called Battle of Britain Sunday for the loss of fifty-six of its bombers and fighters. The RAF lost twenty-eight fighters with twelve pilots killed, twelve wounded and one being taken prisoner of war. The German bombers had managed to get through to London but at a terrible cost. They did cause damage to the railway lines (but rail traffic was only disrupted for three days) whilst the Docks had got away unscathed. The day from the German viewpoint was a failure, having failed to achieve any of their primary aims whilst suffering a great cost in human lives and aircraft lost. The RAF had proven yet again it was not a spent force and had succeeded in thwarting the major German daylight attack of the Battle of Britain. German bombing raids by daylight were failing and increasingly the bombing switched to attacks by night; four days later, Adolf Hitler postponed the invasion of the United Kingdom indefinitely. However, despite the experiences of 15 September 1940, the Battle of Britain was still not regarded as over.

Understandably, the days that followed 15 September 1940 were much quieter for the German bombers which did not appear in force over Great Britain until 18 September. However, German reconnaissance aircraft were as active as usual, whilst to the north German seaplanes were particularly active and suffered two losses during 16 September:

Leutnant **Clemens Lucas, 3/***Kue.Fl.Gr* **506**

We were based at Stavanger–Sola seadrome. We had been briefed to torpedo a tanker of 8,000–10,000 GRT sailing south from the Moray Firth, escorted by two small destroyers. The reconnaissance plane had reported a speed of 10-knots.

At about 2300 hrs [on 15 September] we saw the tanker north of the Isle of May. Very low, we flew a wide turn and waited until the ship was in front of the Isle. Then it turned into the southern entrance and soon the full moon was seen to the north-west. In case of anti-aircraft fire, we attacked at low level. About 500m ahead of the ship, I climbed to 50m, aimed at the middle of the ship using my night sights as well as an angle of allowance, pressed the button on the right of my control column and released the torpedo. Now I had to fly straight ahead for thirty seconds so that our slipstream would not affect the torpedo. The tanker's speed had been about 3 or 4 knots – not much wake could be seen. The depth of the torpedo was set at 6m. After dropping the torpedo, I immediately went down to 10m altitude and saw that the tanker had been hit amidships.

However, both destroyer's pom-poms had already fired their first salvoes. Both of our engines were hit and stopped working. I was able to land on the sea without any problems – it was 0035 hrs in the morning of 16 September. Our *Bordfunker* [*Fw* Erich Kalinowski] fixed a drogue anchor to both floats to stabilise the plane. When two small grey fishing boats appeared at about 0400 hrs, we scuttled our aircraft. How? After we had set off two incendiary bombs, we took to our dinghy and ten minutes later the plane sank. The British fishermen took us on board and we gave them our dinghy as a present. Then they put us ashore at a small fishing port.

The He 115 of Lt *Lucas is brought ashore despite sinking.* (via Watkins)

At about 0800 hrs, we were picked up by two Jeeps commanded by an officer of a Scottish Regiment based in Edinburgh. We were treated very well and at the Officers' Mess, we got a rich breakfast. After two days we were transported to an interrogation centre at Cockfosters near London. In Germany we had been told already that there would be questioning so we remained silent. We only had our private identity cards with us on which were our parents' addresses. After three days, my parents got the information via the Swiss Consulate that we were alive.

The second Heinkel 115 to be lost fell victim not as a result of enemy action but, and not for the first time during the summer of 1940, the weather:

Leutnant zur See Hans Otto Aldus, *1/Kue.Fl.Gr* 906

Our mission began at the seadrome of Norderney and our task was an armed reconnaissance of the Scottish east coast. The outward and return flight would have lasted five hours which allowed us to stay for a good two hours on the reconnaissance, including a necessary safety factor. Enough time in good weather, even at night.

The weather proved to be crucial. Because of sketchy meteorological reports from the west, the forecast was inaccurate. We were caught in deteriorating weather – rain showers, low cloud and bad visibility. A fast approaching depression. Because it was approaching so quickly, we believed that it was a local, temporary depression and that the weather over our reconnaissance area would possibly be better.

Left to right Uffz Meissner, LtzS *Aldus and their usual pilot named Rethage.* (Aldus)

We did not abort the flight, particularly because from time to time the moon broke through the clouds and was reflected in the water. However, as we approached the coast near to Peterhead (by dead

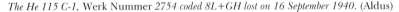

The He 115 C-1, Werk Nummer *2754 coded 8L+GH lost on 16 September 1940.* (Aldus)

A He 115 of 1/906 is brought back on land after another mission, Rugen, early 1940. (Aldus)

reckoning and radio direction finding) there was no visibility at all. I think that I can still remember that we saw some lights and we were shot at. In these poor conditions, we could not carry out our orders and so we turned back towards the sea. During this turn, one wing tip touched the ground resulting in an unintentional forced-landing! For me it meant serious injuries and I still suffer the after effects. For all three of us it meant captivity.

As far as I can remember, we stayed at a farmhouse for the rest of the night. I was then taken to a hospital in Aberdeen and after a month to a military hospital at Edinburgh. After five months I had recovered from my injuries and was taken to the prisoner of war camp at Shap Wells. I was eventually released in November 1946 when I returned to my home country.

The weather improved sufficiently on 18 September 1940 which allowed the Germans to commit one of its bomber units recently brought into action in the Battle of Britain. Originally a Dornier 17 unit, KG 77 was converting to the Junkers 88 for much of August and early September 1940.

Unfortunately, on its first major daylight attack in the afternoon of 18 September, the RAF taught III/KG 77 a severe lesson. Briefed to attack London and Tilbury Docks, nine Junkers 88s were shot down, including that of the *Gruppen Kommandeur Maj* Max Kless.

Again, the days that followed 18 September 1940 were hampered by poor weather and a lack (or unwillingness?) of German bombers in daylight and it must be said that the remainder of September, and October for that matter, were an anti-climax compared to 15 September. On the 21st of the month, a rare German aircraft, a Dornier 215, fell victim to a Spitfire pilot ostensibly on rest with his Squadron near Liverpool:

The badge of KG 77, a unit regarded by many as an unlucky Geschwader.

Believed to be Ju 88 A-1, Werk Nummer 7092 *coded 9K+MR of 7/KG 51 after its crash-landing at Lille–Nord, 20 September 1940.* (Hoehler)

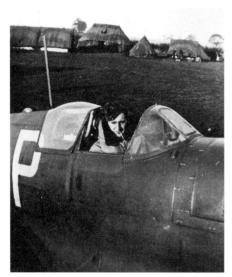

Plt Off Dennis Adams, 611 Sqn, November 1939.
(Adams)

Pilot Officer Dennis Adams, Green 2, 'B' Flight, 611 Squadron

I was ordered off from Ringway at 1630 hrs to investigate a Bogey at 20,000ft over Liverpool. I scrambled to this height and was then ordered to 25,000ft. On reaching this height, anti-aircraft fire started to burst around me and chase me and on looking up, I saw the enemy aircraft directly above me travelling east at about 220mph. On sighting me climbing up behind, the enemy aircraft turned west into the sun. On reaching a position approximately 450 yards astern, the enemy aircraft opened fire at me. I swung out to the right and did a beam attack on his starboard side, firing a five second burst. Immediately, a stream of coolant or petrol came from the starboard engine and the rear gunner ceased firing (enemy fire ineffective). I then went astern of the enemy aircraft and fired a longish burst at 250 yards closing to approximately 150 yards. The port engine then emitted brown smoke or oil vapour and stopped. The enemy aircraft continued in a westerly direction, losing height, and finally crashed in a field...

Leutnant Rolf Book, *Aufkl.Gr.Ob.dL.*

We took off from Caen that 21 September 1940. We entered British airspace at altitude of approximately 27,000ft near Plymouth on our way to Liverpool. The sky was cloudy and I had my doubts whether we could be able to take pictures over Liverpool. However, the sky cleared and we were able to take pictures for about twelve minutes. Apparently we entered British airspace without being identified by radar. I take this from the fact that we got no warning from our side which usually monitored communications between British fighters and the ground stations. On our way back from Liverpool, we suddenly noticed the fighter behind and above us, approaching very fast. Unfortunately (for us!) we couldn't do very much as our guns 'went on strike' after a few shots and the rest was inevitable. We couldn't bale out as *Uffz* Pelzer had been mortally wounded after the first attack and so we made a forced-landing – not too bad I think. As a result, I was guest of His Majesty for six years and two months.

The days that followed saw an increase in aggressive sweeps by Messerschmitt 109s and the occasional fighter bomber attack against London. Bomber operations were very much limited to the occasional daylight nuisance attack against specific targets or mainly night attacks. Surviving logbooks from this period bear this out. For example, *Oblt* Erwin Moll, a pilot with 4/KG 76 flew his last daylight mission against Great Britain on 15 September 1940 and from then until the end of the Battle of Britain flew nine night-time attacks purely against London. *Uffz* Herbert Schick, a *Bordfunker* with 3/KGr 100 first flew against England on the night of the 13/14 August 1940 and flew a total of sixteen bombing missions, all of them by night, before he and his crew were returned to Germany at the end of September 1940. After 8 September 1940, all of his flights (nine in total) were against London. Both Moll and Schick were shot down and taken prisoners of war in 1941 during night attacks against London.

24 September 1940 would see another minor change in tactics by the Germans. A few bombers were briefed to attack London early that morning but turned back, either because of weather or the threat of fighters, before reaching the target. Then, just after lunch, the fighter bombers of *Erprobungsgruppe* 210 carried out the first of two attacks against the Supermarine Factory near Southampton.

Uffz *Herbert Schick*. (Schick)

The first attack, which took place at 1330 hrs, succeeded in damaging the factory, not badly enough to stop production of the Spitfire but resulting in the deaths of forty-two, most of whom worked at the factory. Another attack was carried out three hours later but was ineffectual. This time one of the fighter bombers was lost in addition to two of the escorting fighters; reports state that the German losses were attributable to anti-aircraft fire but it now seems likely that Spitfires of 609 Squadron were to blame:

Pilot Officer David Crook, 609 Squadron

As we were climbing over the Isle of Wight at about 25,000ft, we sighted the German bombers some distance away to the south, a great mass of machines coming steadily on in very good formation. Above them, ranging up to about 35,000ft, the Me 109s were circling round and round so that every now and then I could see a quick flash as their wings caught the sun. They were watching us like cats, just waiting to attack the bombers and then the fun would start and it would be the usual hair-raising competition to see if we could get the bombers before the 109s got to us.

The CO swung 'B' Flight into echelon starboard and prepared to do a beam attack. God, I thought, now for it. In that instant somebody shouted "Look out, 109s!" and I whipped round just as a whole pack of Messerschmitts tore over our heads not more than 30ft above us. They came down at a terrific speed out of the sun and we never saw them at all until they were on us. We split up in all directions, diving and turning to avoid them. I went down about 2,000ft and then looked round and saw a few Spitfires forming up again and chasing some Dorniers [sic] over the Isle of Wight. I went after them as hard as I could but was about half a mile behind and as we were all going flat out I didn't seem to get much nearer.

One Dornier was rather behind the rest of the Hun formation and two black streaks of smoke from his engines showed that he realised his danger and was doing everything he could to catch up. A moment later the leading Spitfire (I learned later that it was Sgt Feary) opened fire on the Dornier and gave him a long burst. The bomber flew steadily on for a moment and then he turned slowly over on his back and started to spin down. We all watched him; it was rather a shaking sight. Down he went, spinning faster and faster at an incredible rate for such a big machine and then suddenly a wing was wrenched off. The Dornier gave a lurch and continued to dive but now turning crazily over and over. The crew must have all been dead inside the cabin for nobody got out. I saw the other wing and tail break away and the fuselage then went straight down like a stone and disappeared from sight. A moment later, looking down, I saw a patch of foam appear on the sea over 20,000ft below showing where he had dropped...[7]

Sgt Alan Feary (left) relates the combat to the Squadron Intelligence Officer.

[7] As normally happened, Messerschmitt 110s were mistaken for Dornier 17s and no Dornier 17s took part in this attack. Claims should therefore have been filed for three Messerschmitt 110s by Plt Off John Curchin, Plt Off Mike Staples and Sgt Alan Feary.

On 25 September 1940, London again had a brief rest from the daylight attention of the German bombers. Whether the Germans thought that the RAF fighters were concentrated around London thus leaving other potential targets relatively undefended is not known but the only major attack of the day was by the Heinkel 111s of KG 55 against the Bristol Aircraft Factory at Filton near Bristol (with *Erprobungsgruppe* 210 carrying out a diversionary attack against Portland).

He 111 of 3/KG 55. (Kaufhold)

Because of an error by the RAF controllers, the German bombers made it to their target unmolested. They succeeded in stopping aircraft production at the factory and causing in excess of 350 casualties but then the RAF fighters managed to intercept, shooting down four bombers and one of the Messerschmitt 110 escorts:

Unteroffizier **Rudolf Weisbach, 1/KG 55**

We were based at Villacoublay near Paris and the order was to attack the Bristol Aircraft Factory. In the morning, at about 1000 hrs, another *Geschwader* flew a light attack against London which hopefully would draw off the British fighters. At 1100 hrs, we took off, headed for Cherbourg and across the Channel for Bristol. Our escort was a *Geschwader* of Bf 109s which after an hour was replaced by a Bf 110 *Geschwader*.

Initially, we met with little opposition – as we approached the target, we encountered fierce *Flak* but then, after we had dropped our bombs, we saw the first Spitfire [sic] and they attacked immediately. During one of the attacks, we lost an engine (the oil supply was hit) and then could not set the pitch of the propeller. We were flying in formation at 5,000m and could not keep up so we dropped as much ballast as possible in the hope that we could reach the French coast on one engine. We then became the target of three to five Spitfires; I cannot say if there were any Hurricanes.

The Channel was very close just as another attack hit the second engine. At the height we were, there was no option but to ditch near Studland but because *Uffz* Altrichter was wounded, our pilot carried out a comparatively good crash-landing on land.[8]

After landing, we tried to get the wounded Altrichter out of the

THIS AND NEXT PAGE *The 1/KG 55 He 111 at Studland, 25 September 1940.* (via Cornwell)

aircraft. Then, as the aircraft was relatively undamaged despite the crash-landing, we planned to set the aircraft on fire. However, we were approached by some civilians from a house 500m away. They

[8] The destruction of this aircraft was jointly credited to Plt Offs John Wigglesworth of 238 Squadron and John Curchin of 609 Squadron.

were armed and took away our pistols. Some ten minutes later, a lady brought some tea for the wounded – the pilot [*Fw* Fritz Juerges] and the gunner [*Uffz* Otto Mueller] had been slightly injured in the landing but Altrichter had been badly wounded in the thigh. After ten minutes, a military vehicle approached and we were all taken away but it was too late for Altrichter; he had bled to death.

A He 111 of KG 55 shows the after effects of an RAF fighter attack.

Whether the Germans were encouraged by the attack on Bristol is not known but the following day KG 55 and *Erprobungsgruppe* 210 attacked the Supermarine Factory again. This attack was also successful, succeeding in stopping the production of Spitfires and causing over 100 casualties. German losses were light – just one of the bombers and two of the Messerschmitt 110 escorts; a reconnaissance Messerschmitt 110 of 4(F)/14 was shot down by Flt Lt William Blackadder of 607 Squadron just after the attack, presumably tasked with assessing the effectiveness of the earlier attack. The RAF claimed to have shot down thirty-three German aircraft – a clear case of over optimism and over claiming, especially as five of their fighters were either shot down or written off (twelve of them being claimed by JG 2 who were escorting the bombers).

The German tactics changed again on 27 September when the Germans returned to their 'rolling' attacks. Preceded by a *Freie Jagd*, eighty or so heavily escorted Junkers 88s of I and II/KG 77 headed towards London only to receive the same punishment meted out to III/KG 77 on 18 September 1940. Four Junkers 88s were shot down (and a further eight were lost in a similar attack later in the afternoon) and the Messerschmitt 110 escort was similarly mauled.

Meanwhile, back to the west another attack was about to take place against the Parnall Aircraft Factory at Yate near Bristol by the apparently indefatigable *Erprobungsgruppe* 210. This time the RAF fighters were in the right place at the right time in great numbers. The attack was broken up and four fighter bombers, including those flown by the *Gruppen Kommandeur Hptm* Martin Lutz and the *Staffel Kapitaen* of 2 *Staffel*, *Oblt* Wilhelm-Richard Roessiger, were shot down; both of these officers were posthumously awarded the *Ritterkreuz*.

28 September was a day of relative rest for the bomber crews. They had been active during the hours of darkness but only a few Junkers 88s were committed to daylight attacks on London under a very heavy escort. The German fighters did particularly well on what was a very costly day for Fighter Command, accounting for seventeen British fighters; only two German aircraft (both of them Messerschmitt 109s) were lost in combat throughout the hours of daylight. 29 September was similarly quiet for the Germans and a better day for Fighter Command. The only incident of note took place during the early evening when Heinkel 111s from all three *Staffeln* of III/KG 55 attacked Liverpool Docks. Wary of what had happened to the *Geschwader* and other units over the west of Great Britain during the past week, the formation scouted around the coast up the Irish Sea, close to neutral Eire. Eleven Hurricanes from 79 Squadron based at Pembrey in South Wales were scrambled to intercept and as the sun began to set, they spotted the German bombers. Aircraft from 7 and 8 *Staffeln* had managed to slip past undetected but 9/KG 55 was unfortunate enough to be attacked. One Heinkel 111 flown by *Oblt* Hans Kohler was shot down and another two returned damaged, one

aircraft having all of its crew wounded. The German gunners did well though, shooting down the Hurricanes of Plt Off George Nelson-Edwards and Fg Off George Peters, the latter being killed; a third Hurricane, flown by Fg Off Paul Mayhew, landed in Eire and was impounded.

On 30 September 1940, it appeared that the Germans threw all caution to the wind; it was also destined to be the day which saw the last major daylight bombing attacks on Great Britain during the Battle of Britain and, for that matter, the remainder of the war.

Using their tried and tested 'rolling' attacks, the first major attack did not materialise until early in the afternoon when a large, heavily escorted formation was plotted heading for London. This was successfully intercepted and, although few German bombers were shot down, the remainder were turned back:

Oberleutnant **Fritz Oeser, 2/KG 77**

That morning, I received [the gift of] an ashtray which I took to be a bad omen. Before the mission to London, I had to instruct *Uffz* Klasing, the stand-in *Bordmechaniker*, how to handle the job of a *Bordmechaniker* and gunner because every pilot had to fly on this day and we were short of *Bordmechanikers*. Finally, flying in formation to the target, I was not happy when one engine cut out at 6,000ft over the Channel and I had to break away from the formation and leave my seat to see what the trouble was. I quickly found out that a switch was set incorrectly in the *Bordmechaniker*'s area – the engine ran again and I caught up again abeam the British south coast.

According to our information, we were sure that the mission would be one of the last as we had been told that "riots in London against the continuation of the war were at such a state that the police and Army could not keep control any longer." However, about 20 miles from London at 18,000ft, the British fighters were diving from 30,000ft into our formation, opening fire and continuing downwards. They managed to break up the formation. The result for me was one engine cooler out, oxygen bottles damaged, the greenhouse front left side without perspex, the rear upper machine gun out of action and the *Bordmechaniker* seriously wounded. I got an explosive bullet in the left shoulder and another caused a wide wound above my right eye.

Veering away from the formation, I ordered the bombs be dropped and we dived to ground level in the hope of escaping. Some minutes later, two fighters intercepted and tried to shoot us down. My only chance was to watch the attackers and by turning towards them when they were in an attacking position. Finally, one of the fighters turned off but the other one carried out another two attacks and obviously ran out of ammunition. He then began flying very closely in formation with me to see what had happened in the cockpit. Then he too disappeared.

Suddenly, near the ground, another fighter appeared and attacked – we were only flying at 100ft at this time. My aircraft was scarcely manoeuvrable and flying at 100-knot and then the second engine was hit and began burning. My only chance was a 30° turn to right to search for a field for a forced-landing. Before that, I had to fly over a large tree but failed – it smashed into the belly but I was still able to touch down in an almost perfect belly landing on Gatwick Racecourse...

Sergeant Paul Farnes, Yellow 3, 'A' Flight, 501 Squadron

I was on patrol with the Squadron who were ordered to climb to 20,000ft. I stayed with the Squadron to 14,000ft but then I was so cold that I decided to leave; the reason for this was the fact that my hood had jammed fully open. I came down through clouds about five miles west-south-west of Gatwick and commenced to return to base. I got to about eight miles north of Gatwick when I sighted a Ju 88, diving rapidly but not steeply, which was emitting a thin trail of white smoke so I assumed it had been damaged in a previous attack. The enemy aircraft was heading south so I turned through 180°, pulled the plug and commenced to chase him. We were then at 4,000ft. I overhauled him at Gatwick and was about to attack him when he turned towards me. I continued my attack from slightly head on, continuing to fire until I broke away 20 yards behind his tail. I turned to make another attack but could not see him. At that moment, I saw several vehicles driving across Gatwick aerodrome and looking at the direction they were going, I saw that the enemy aircraft had crash-landed on Gatwick Racecourse. After I had landed at Gatwick, I was informed by eye witnesses that after my attack, both engines had caught fire, emitting black smoke, and enemy aircraft had force-landed immediately after.

Oberleutnant Fritz Oeser

...I ordered the crew to leave the aircraft and to activate the incendiary bomb under my seat. At that moment, one of the crew at the front of the aircraft stopped this intention, stating that the hood couldn't be moved. However, when the cockpit cleared of smoke, I saw about thirty soldiers about 200 yards away. After about five minutes, they fired three warning shots into the aircraft to try and make us come out, not knowing that we were not able to do that. Maybe they assumed we were daredevils! However, shortly after that, we were taken prisoner and taken away.

A final attack in the east on that day occurred just after 1600 hrs when another formation of Junkers 88s again headed for London together

Fritz Oeser's Ju 88 on display after its crash-landing. (via Cornwell)

with a heavy escort of Messerschmitt 109s. The formation was broken up and the resultant combats ranged from Kent almost into eastern Hampshire. However, no bombers were shot down and the losses were suffered just by the fighters.

As that attack in the east was coming to a close, another was developing in the west when forty-three Heinkel 111s of I and II/KG 55 tried to attack the Westland Factory at Yeovil in Somerset whilst eleven Junkers 88s of I/KG 51 carried out a diversionary attack on Southampton. A similar situation to what had happened on 27 September and in the east of Britain earlier on 30 September occurred when the formation, hampered by bad weather, was intercepted and turned back. Sadly, the Heinkel 111s unknowingly dropping their bombs on the helpless town of Shaftesbury. German bomber losses were predictable – KG 55 lost four bombers with twelve aircrew killed and six wounded. Four of the wounded, which included *Maj Dr* Ernst Kuhl, Operations Officer of KG 55, were picked up from the Channel; Kuhl would later become *Geschwader Kommodore* of KG 55 and was destined to receive the *Ritterkreuz mit Eichenlaub*. Even the diversionary attack by I/KG 51 lost an aircraft when the Junkers 88 of *Fw* Fritz Paczinski of 1 *Staffel* was shot down into the sea off Selsey Bill by Red Section of 602 Squadron; there were no survivors from the crew of four.

The deciding month of the Battle of Britain was over as far as daylight bombing operations were concerned and the RAF had emerged the victor, not just on the final day of the month but on almost each of the preceding twenty-nine days. The *Luftwaffe* still had the might but had failed to press home any advantage that it had won. Furthermore, weather, bad luck, tactical errors, the sheer guts of the RAF fighter pilots and the hard work of the supporting ground crews had very much influenced the outcome. It was true that the German fighters had managed to wrest air superiority from Fighter Command for much of the first six days of the month but then their tactics and aims changed. Air superiority was then lost by the Germans which allowed the RAF's vengeance to be wreaked on many of the bomber crews and their aircraft for the rest of the month.

After 15 September 1940, German bombers flew more and more operations by night which gave greater protection to the bombers and their crews, especially the Dornier 17 and Heinkel 111 which had proved to be very vulnerable against day fighters. It had been hoped that the newer and faster Junkers 88 could rely on its greater speed and manoeuvrability but was still no match for Spitfires and Hurricanes unless heavily protected by the Messerschmitt 109. However, the problem with the Messerschmitt 109 was its limited range and the Messerschmitt 110 had been proved to be woefully inadequate as a long-range fighter.

The last ten days of September 1940 had seen a sudden increase in fighter-bomber operations by single-seat fighters which was ironic as the premier German fighter-bomber unit, *Erprobungsgruppe* 210, had on 27 September 1940 suffered badly at the hands of the RAF. The final month of the Battle of Britain would now see a dramatic reduction in German daylight bombing operations and a greater switch to night time operations and much of the death and glory would be experienced by the German day-fighter and fighter-bomber pilots.

4
Anti-Climax
– October 1940

After the carnage of the previous three months, October 1940 was very much a let down and relief for the German bomber crews. Because of the switch to night operations and the onset of winter with its associated poor weather, major daylight attacks only took place on two days during October 1940 with the German bombers preferring to carry out single nuisance attacks. Even then, they were vulnerable:

Oberleutnant Hans Langer, *Staffel Kapitaen Stab*/KG 2

After trying hard, I managed to get the permission from my *Kommodore*, *Oberst* Johannes Fink, to attack targets by single aircraft in daylight. On 2 October 1940, there was a 6/10ths layer of cloud over Great Britain. This type of weather, using the cloud banks as cover, suited single-aircraft attacks so we took off, the crew consisting of myself as pilot, *Oblt* Erich Eitze as *Beobachter*, *Uffz* Robert Seidel as *Bordfunker* and *Uffz* Hellmut Bellmann as *Bordmechaniker*. The target was the Handley Page Aircraft Factory near London. We set course and climbed just above the broken cloud layer at an altitude of about 2,000m. Just before 1000 hrs, we reached the southern suburbs of London – the enormous city was lying under a layer of haze but only a few small clouds disrupted the blue of the sky. I thought it would be senseless to carry on so I changed course back for the Channel.

Oblt *Erich Eitze*, Oblt *Hans Langer and* Lt *Heinrich Hunger; Hunger was later awarded the* Ritterkreuz *only to be killed in action over Russia on 14 August 1941.* (Langer)

After a few minutes, the *Bordfunker* shouted over the intercom "Fighters from starboard and behind!" – the height of the cloud base had decreased as well as the number of clouds so it was difficult for me to find somewhere to shelter from the attacking British fighters – three

Hurricanes. The first hits struck my plane. The *Beobachter* and *Bordfunker* tried to fend off the attacking fighters with their machine guns. It was difficult to aim at the fighters and then they attacked head on. By then it was hopeless to try and find shelter in the clouds and I was forced to descend and fly at low level. Then a salvo hit the instrument panel and the port engine began to emit black smoke, slight at first but then becoming thicker. Now there were only two Hurricanes left – the third one must have broken off due to lack of fuel. There was no hope of escaping so I gave the order to bale out. I unfastened my seat belt but I was touched on the shoulder and heard the *Bordmechaniker* say "My parachute has been torn." In the meantime, we were only at 80m altitude, the plane was losing speed and I could only control the plane by gliding. I withdrew the order to bale out.

Only one fighter was now circling close above the Dornier 17. With frightening speed, the ground got closer and closer and we could just make out an almost rectangular field. Suddenly, the *Beobachter* heard me shout "I'm not strapped in!" – the plane would crash-land in the next few minutes. Nevertheless, Erich Eitze unfastened his belt and fastened mine. At the last second, we were all ready and moments later the Do 17 touched the ground, sliding along on its belly, undercarriage retracted. I succeeded in side-slipping past a large pylon and no sooner had the plane come to a halt than the *Bordfunker* rushed out to destroy papers detailing call signs and radio frequencies.[1] Everybody feared that the plane would explode – in great haste, I struggled to get my flying helmet and microphone off but heard Erich Eitze's calm voice saying "Just a moment, I will do it" and cut through the cord with his utility knife saying "Now we can get out as we are guests of the English King!" Quickly, we left the immediate vicinity of our good 'kite', completely astonished and relieved that we had survived. It was 1028 hrs; the dogfight had lasted twenty-eight minutes – an eternity for those involved...

The lone Dornier 17 had the misfortune to be spotted by five pilots from 17 Squadron who were returning from patrol, low on fuel. Plt Off Frantisek Fajtl, Fg Off Howard 'Cowboy' Blatchford, Plt Off Jack Ross, Plt Off Leonard Stevens and Flt Lt Alfred Bayne were all credited with the kill:

Flight Lieutenant Alfred Bayne, Blue 1, 'B' Flight, 17 Squadron

I was leading 17 Squadron when we were vectored to intercept bandits as we were returning from patrol. I first sighted the Do 17 eight

---

[1] *Uffz* Seidel had experienced being shot down before (on 27 May 1940 south of Dunkirk) so was well versed in what to do this time.

Hans Langer's Do 17 before…

…and after the crash-landing. (Langer)

miles north-east of Colchester at 4,000–5,000ft in and out of 8/10ths cloud. I eventually engaged just over Harwich with a rear attack in a break in cloud, opening at 300 yards and diving to 200 yards giving a ten second burst. Return fire was noticed from the rear top gun which stopped after a big flash from the port side of the fuselage near the cockpit. Enemy aircraft then went into cloud and I found him again over Ipswich and gave him the rest of my ammunition in another Number 1 attack at the same range. I then returned to base to rearm and refuel having been airborne for two hours. My Numbers 2 and 3 also attacked the enemy aircraft after separating from me.

The other pilots witnessed the crash-landing and headed for base very low on fuel. Both Fg Off Blatchford and Plt Off Fajtl force-landed in fields near Pulham; Plt Off Jack Ross didn't get much further than the field next to the crash-landed German bomber:

Oberleutnant Hans Langer

…Suddenly, we noticed a Hurricane which landed in the field a few metres away. A very young *Leutnant* climbed down from his plane, approached us, stood to attention in front of me, saluted and said "Congratulations Sir; you have given me a good fight. I've only got minutes of fuel left. Let's shake hands!" Still confused and angry, I replied "Three against one is not a fair combat!" to which he turned his back on me and walked back to his plane.

A few minutes later, some armed Home Guard appeared at the edge of the field. With the words "Hands up!" they told us to surrender. In the middle of enemy territory, resistance would be insane so we handed over our pistols. It wasn't long before a lorry with regular troops appeared and we were taken to a nearby village and put into a barrack-like building. There, us officers were separated from the NCOs – unfortunately we heard nothing further from them for the rest of our captivity.

Towards the evening, we were eventually taken to a dark, garage-like room where some time later, we got something to eat – two dried fish on a metal plate. We ate using our hands and slowly our fear and excitement faded away. We managed a sound, dreamless sleep, not waking until the next morning. Then we were given a cup of tea and some biscuits and soon we were sitting on a lorry again which took us to the train station. There the escorting officer, a Lieutenant, turned to me and said "You take my coat." I said that I would not wear the coat of my enemy to which he said "You will see." As soon as we entered the station, a large crowd recognised us as Germans and shouted "German baby killers!" Cold shivers ran through both of us but an escorting soldier wielding his rifle in a semi-circle and a Bobby, with his truncheon, fended off the more aggressive civilians and the officer followed with pistol drawn. Finally, we got into a First Class carriage where we were pushed in and the door locked. At the windows, people were shaking their fists at us but we could not hear their raging yells any more.

With unspeakable relief, both of us sank into the upholstered seats. The fear of the last few minutes had been harder to endure than the strain of the half hour dogfight. Eventually the train left the station and we suddenly got another fright when the escorting officer sitting directly opposite draws his pistol. In bewilderment, we feared the worse but he said "Being armed myself, I do not want to be faced by unarmed men." Whilst saying this, he removed the bullets from his revolver and put them into his pocket. A true, knightly gesture.

The first major daylight raid of the month by conventional bombers (as opposed to fighter-bombers) took place on 7 October when II/KG 51 attacked the Westland Aircraft Factory at Yeovil. The bombers succeeded in reaching the target, harried all the way by RAF fighters but the damage caused was not that severe, even though

Hans Langer photographed at Euston Station, 3 October 1940. (Langer)

there were over 100 casualties. The Germans lost seven of the escorting Messerschmitt 110s, this aircraft making its last appearance over Great Britain en masse for the remainder of the war during this attack. The fighter losses could have been higher if it was not for the intervention of JG 2 which claimed at least eight RAF fighters. Nevertheless, just one bomber was shot down:

Oberleutnant **Sigurd Hey, 5/KG 51**

I had flown twelve missions against England, all of them but this one being flown by night. On this day, we took off from the normal II/KG 51 base at Orly; most of the night missions took off from Villeroche where we had installed an artificial horizon to help night take-offs.

Being a former instrument flying instructor, I was normally selected for night raids. I volunteered to fly this day as one of the pilots had been taken ill and as the wings of my aircraft were being modified by a Junkers Field Service team at Villacoublay, I took his plane and called for my crew in a hurry. We got airborne as one of the last of about twenty-five Junkers 88s and got a position on the edge of the formation.

Oblt *Sigurd Hey*. (Hey)

We arrived over Cherbourg where the Bf 109s had already been waiting for us for half an hour. They escorted us to the British coast and had to return because they were all low on fuel. Thus our only fighter escort from now on was made up from Bf 110s – no protection against thirty or forty Spitfires and Hurricanes now coming from all directions.

I was hit in the radiator on my starboard engine. Although I dropped my 500 kilogram bomb immediately and I feathered the damaged engine, I could not hold my position in the formation and began to lag behind. I therefore turned southwards, diving a few thousand feet and tried to reach the French coast on only one engine.

Then three Spitfires came, attacking from all angles. At first a hit in the controls forced me to hold the aircraft straight and level just by using the trim wheel. Next, the fuselage tank was hit and the aircraft caught fire. It was then that I gave the order to bale out but I received no reply because the three of them had already left because of the dense smoke. When the aircraft went into a flat spin, I was lucky to get out and landed safely by parachute where I was quickly taken prisoner by two old men with shotguns.

A number of RAF fighters, both Spitfires and Hurricanes, claimed to have shot down this bomber but the following, given by a Hurricane pilot, gives a good account of what happened:

Pilot Officer Robert Doe, Yellow 1, 'A' Flight, 238 Squadron

...At 20,000ft over Warmwell, Me 109s carried out a head on attack. The Squadron split up. I dived straight for the lower bombers which were straggling considerably and attacked a Ju 88 from astern, opening fire at 300 yards. The first burst stopped the starboard engine. Overtaking speed was very high so I half-rolled upwards and attacked the enemy aircraft from above with a short burst at 100 yards. I broke away and carried out a beam attack from the port side from 300 yards. Enemy aircraft turned away and started diving. As it dived, a burst of fire appeared in front of the tail which flew off. Three people baled out and the enemy aircraft crashed in flames 6 miles north of Maiden Newton.

As the month continued, despite many bitter air battles between fighters and fighter-bombers, no further major daylight raids took place. The pendulum of battle had clearly swung to night time operations with the German bombers being further aided by precision Very High Frequency

A He 111 of KGr 100 – clearly visible on the fuselage are the three aerial masts associated with X-Verfahren. (Schick)

radio beam navigation and bombing systems such as *Knickebein* and the Very High Frequency multi-beam and single beam precision bombing systems known as *X-Verfahren* and *Y-Verfahren* respectively. As yet, the RAF had no answer to this and the first airborne radar-assisted kill was still over a month off. Nevertheless, a number of German bombers were being lost at night as a result of anti-aircraft fire. However, for the moment losses were very light.

There was still the occasional daylight battle with the occasional surprising result. For instance, 92 Squadron definitely came off the loser in a combat with a Dornier 17 of 1/KG 2 on the morning of 10 October 1940. The Spitfires of Plt Offs John Drummond and Desmond Williams collided during what appeared to be a one-sided combat and both pilots were killed. Then one of the Dornier 17s gunners damaged the Spitfire flown by Sgt Walter Ellis forcing him to force-land and writing off his Spitfire in the process. The Dornier 17 returned safely albeit its pilot, *Lt* Walter Dilcher was killed.

This Ju 88 A-1 coded 9K+HS of 8/KG 51 was shot down by AA fire in the early hours of 10 October 1940 whilst bombing London; Uffz Richard Metschuldt and his crew were taken prisoner. (Wildermuth)

Another daylight combat took place over the Irish Sea on 11 October 1940. Three Dornier 17s of *Kuestenfliegergruppe* 606 were part of a force briefed to attack Liverpool Docks. Two Squadrons were scrambled to intercept the German bombers. It is believed that the Hurricanes of 312 Squadron damaged one of the bombers, two of its crew baling out whilst the bomber continued back to France where it crash-landed badly damaged. Two other Dornier 17s were shot down by Spitfires of 611 Squadron:

Leutnant zur See **Juergen Von Krause, 1/*Kue.Fl.Gr* 606**

On 11 October 1940, our target was again Liverpool Docks. Flying height was 4,000–5,000m and the size of our formation in between *Staffel* and *Gruppe*. We were attacked by RAF fighters (Spitfires) just before and after the target.

My Dornier 17 had dropped back a little behind the formation and logically was the first aircraft to be attacked. I can remember a series of hits caused problems with one engine. Consequently, we lost contact with the rest of the

Lt zS Juergen von Krause. (von Krause)

formation, turned further out to sea to the west and dived. However, two Spitfires stayed close. We hit one of them and perhaps it was shot down but the other one finished us off. After the second engine had seized up, we had to ditch. The aircraft sank immediately and we were lucky to get out in time and inflate our life jackets. After some time, I found our dinghy – I was able to inflate it using the compressed air and after a few hours, we were picked up by a Dutch patrol boat which took us to Holyhead...

Again, the RAF did not come away from these combats without incident. The Hurricane flown by Plt Off Josef Jaske of 312 Squadron was badly damaged by exploding bullets in the fabric and spars of the main and tail planes, elevators and aileron. Sgt Ken Pattison of 611 Squadron is thought to have got lost and was killed whilst trying to force-land near Kidderminster whilst *Lt zS* Krause was correct in saying he thought that they had damaged one of the Spitfires that attacked them:

Pilot Officer Thomas Draper Williams, Yellow Section, 611 Squadron

The Germans had started night bombing Merseyside and they used to send in a few aircraft just before evening to lay incendiaries and markers at last light. Our function was to intercept these aircraft by making a sweep out to Anglesey and back and then landing after last light anywhere we could. One of the more hair-raising experiences was to land at Penrhos near Criccieth.

We were always ordered to take off by telephone or Verey pistol. We were fitted with a Very High Frequency radio which was excellent but did not come into operation until we were about 11,000ft. We used to park down a slope near the guardroom at Ternhill and take off was a little exciting, weaving through the training aircraft doing circuits and bumps.

On 11 October 1940, we were about to take off at about 1800 hrs when we received a telephone message saying that a plot had been received on three-plus aircraft near the Scillies. The message said that if these aircraft continued on their present course, height and speed, they would be over Holyhead at 1830 hrs at 14,000ft.

We had heard this story often before and had been disappointed but we were up sun of Holyhead at 1815 hrs and to our surprise, three Dorniers arrived dead on time. My recollection was that we were six Spitfires and that it was six Dorniers but the entry in my logbook is inconsistent with this and indicates that there were three Dorniers and two of us, Fg Off Ian Hay having returned with engine trouble earlier on.

Fg Off Douglas Watkins (for some reason known as 'Dirty') attacked one Dornier and I followed in behind him. In retrospect, it would have been better if I had attacked a separate aircraft. My hazy recollection was that all the German aircraft were shot down but this seems to be inconsistent with my logbook. Anyway, the aircraft which we attacked immediately turned west, presumably heading for Ireland and we each made two more attacks from the rear.

I had been trained in the Fighter Command Number 1 Attack (an attack from the rear by a single aircraft) to break away by slipping down sideways so as to show the minimum aspect of one's own aircraft to the opposing rear gunner. This I did correctly but Douglas Watkins just got moving quickly by pulling up and to the right, showing the whole belly of his aircraft. In the event, he was not hit at all and I was hit on each of the two attacks. As I was breaking away from the second attack, there was an explosion in the cockpit and it subsequently appeared that I had been hit by an explosive bullet on the underside of the rudder bar. I started to bail out but then realised that the engine was still working and so I got back in and opened up the engine to maximum to obtain the maximum height before it failed, on the assumption that I had been hit either in the oil cooler or in the radiator. However, the aircraft continued to function and on looking around, I saw a ship between Holyhead and Ireland. I flew towards it and circled it at height for some time so that I could, if the engine failed, land beside it or bail out near it.

The engine continued to work with no sign of abnormal temperatures and so I set off for Anglesey. When I reached Anglesey, I looked for somewhere to land and found what appeared to be a suitable field at the south east corner of Anglesey–Bodorgan. I made a dummy approach but found that it was completely obstructed as a defence measure.

I knew that the only flare path in the north west was at Ternhill. I also thought that I would almost certainly crash on landing and it would be unfair to obstruct the flare path whilst other aircraft were in the air. Moreover, it was clear that the aircraft was not handling properly and I did not want to fly over the Welsh mountains at dusk. I accordingly followed the coastline to the Point of Ayr at Prestatyn by which time the plane seemed quite safe, although handling badly. I decided to try and land at Sealand. I knew that there would be no flare path but I knew the district and aerodrome well. My fiancée, later my first wife, was living at Hoylake and accordingly I crossed the River Dee and flew low over her house so that she might guess I might see her later. This caused some concern in the district as they had not had the all clear!

I then flew to Sealand and crossed the aerodrome waggling my wings as best I could as a sign of distress and then did a circuit prior to landing. I selected undercarriage down but it did not work. I then operated the CO2 bottle which is the emergency undercarriage system. I felt some difference in trim but did not get a green light. I then came in to land towards the north-west coming in over the embankment and bridge. Fortunately, the landing was perfectly normal and the undercarriage locked down. I then taxied back to the Duty Pilot's office by which time it was dark. The Duty Pilot was a Flt Lt and I am afraid I asked him in forceful tones where the ambulance and fire tender had been. He explained that they had followed behind on my landing run and had turned back when they saw I was alright. The atmosphere improved and he ended up lending me a Triumph Roadster, a pair of silk pyjamas and a five-gallon coupon for petrol and I duly spent the night at Hoylake.

In retrospect, I think I must have been hit by more than two bullets. The explosive one had broken the main undercarriage and shattered the emergency system and a number of electrical connections. Another one had shot the pitot head away and I was therefore without an airspeed indicator. The third went through the rear spar, splaying it out and jamming the left aileron. Fortunately it also severed the control cable between the ailerons, otherwise they would have both jammed. I was therefore able to partly use the right aileron.

The following day I returned to Ternhill but I gather the aeroplane remained at Sealand for many months before it was repaired.[2] The Dornier, by the way, went into the sea and the three crew were picked up. I hope the rear gunner survived as he continued to fire accurately throughout.

Apart from the odd daylight attack predominantly by Junkers 88s, the rest of the month saw the night offensive continuing. By now, the RAF was trying hard to counter the German night bombers and saw the Boulton Paul Defiant withdrawn from daylight operations at the end of August 1940, being used subsequently as a night fighter. The first Defiant kill by night had occurred on 17/18 September 1940 when Sgts George Laurence and Wilfred Chard of 141 Squadron shot down a Junkers 88 of 3/KG 54. Two days short of a month later, on the night of 15/16 October 1940, a night which saw particularly heavy raids on London and Birmingham, Plt Off Desmond Hughes and Sgt Fred Gash of 264 Squadron shot down a Heinkel 111 of 2/KGr 126 only to overshoot on landing at Luton, damaging their fighter in the process. However, civilian casualties were beginning to rise – the night of 14 October 1940 saw nearly 600 civilian deaths; the night after a further 500 were killed. The Blitz was intensifying and the RAF were helpless for the time being to prevent it from getting even worse.

[2] The repairs to his Spitfire serial P7356 were not completed until 23 February 1941 when the fighter was returned to 611 Squadron. It was eventually written off in an accident on 2 October 1943 whilst with 61 Operational Training Unit.

German reconnaissance aircraft continued to be active in and around Great Britain during October 1940, assessing targets and damage. German losses had been relatively light but on 25 October 1940 RAF fighters met with unusual success:

Plt Off Desmond Hughes (seen here as a Wg Cdr later in the War).

Leutnant **Konrad Wacker, 2(F)/122**

I flew the Bf 110 which was actually a 'destroyer' or heavy fighter. However, our unit used it as a reconnaissance aircraft. An automatic camera had been installed vertically in the fuselage which took a photo every few seconds. The engines had a special supercharger so that we were able to fly at 11,000m.

The problem with the Bf 110 was the short range and that is why I had jettison-able fuel tanks under each wing. Because of these, we could only get to 9,000m before dropping them. So, this was my undoing. During a

Lt Konrad Wacker (in flying helmet) beside the Bf 110 he was flying on 25 October 1940. (Wacker)

Oblt *Schwartz (St Kap)*, Lt *Wacker, unidentified medical officer*, Gefr *Heinrich Gneist*. (Wacker)

reconnaissance flight to the Rolls Royce Factory at Derby, two Spitfires came down on me from a greater height (and out of the sun of course!) and I was handed to them on a plate. By the time I had dropped my tanks (one after the other), one of the engines had been hit. Being a good target for two fighters, the other engine's time soon came and I had no choice but to ditch. My *Bordfunker*, Heinrich Gneist, drowned – I think he had been hit and his life jacket damaged.

Pilot Officer Norman Norfolk, Blue 1, 'B' Flight, 72 Squadron

I was leading Blue Section [Norfolk, Sgt Maurice Pocock and Sgt John White]...I was vectored on 090°, climbing to 25,000ft. Blue 2 sighted enemy aircraft at 1427 hrs flying at 25,000ft due north. I climbed up into the sun to attack but enemy aircraft sighted me and turned to starboard to attack me. His attack was ineffective and I saw no fire. He passed over my head about 20ft above – I then saw the black crosses on the underside of a light blue wing. The upper surface was camouflaged similar to standard markings. After delivering attack, enemy aircraft dived towards the sea, flying south east. I chased enemy aircraft to about 6,000ft, opening fire at 300 yards; from there I closed to 200 yards and after a short burst, an explosion took place in the region of the starboard engine, giving out a long white cloud of smoke which I flew through. I was then too close to enemy aircraft to attack so I broke away to port to avoid collision. Enemy aircraft then went into cloud and after a short search, I returned to base.

Enemy aircraft fired on me at 300 yards but I saw no return fire after my second burst. Only one thing was observed – just before enemy aircraft turned to attack me, he jettisoned an object. To me it seemed square and flat in shape, about five inches in diameter and four foot long. It turned over and over endways, leaving behind a trail of white smoke.

The day after, an armed reconnaissance by a Fw 200 *Condor* of 2/KG 40 flown by *Oblt* Bernhard Jope, had spectacular results. He discovered, bombed and set on fire the liner *Empress of Great Britain*, resulting in the deaths of forty-five passengers. This was the sort of bad news that the British people could do without.

Two days later, it was the turn of a German pilot to be shot down for the second time during the Battle of Britain. Damaged by a British fighter on 28 July 1940, *Oblt* Friedrich-Franz Podbielski, *Staffel Fuehrer* of 9/KG 4, had crash-landed his severely damaged Junkers 88 at Schiphol in Holland. All four crew were wounded, one severely, and Podbielski did not return to duty until 1 October 1940. Even then, he was not allowed to fly.

Later that month, *Reichsmarschall* Goering visited III/KG 4 at Schiphol. A conference followed lunch after which the *Gruppen Kommandeur* of III/KG 4, *Hptm* Erich Bloedorn was appointed *Kommodore* of KG 30 and III/KG 4 was transferred to III/KG 30:

Oberleutnant Friedrich-Franz Podbielski, *Staffel Fuehrer* 7/KG 30

During the conference, I asked Goering if I could fly again and was given command of 7/KG 30.[3] My flight on 27 October 1940 would be my first as *Staffel Fuehrer* and the first after being wounded in July 1940.

On 27 October 1940, we were given the order to carry out Operation OPERNBALL, low level attacks on airfields in England at dusk, using three aircraft from each *Staffel*. After briefing, we flew from Schiphol over the North Sea towards Flamborough Head, low level over Scarborough towards the airfield at Linton-on-Ouse…

RAF Linton-on-Ouse Record Book, 27 October 1940

Linton had its first experience of attack by enemy aircraft. At 1815 hrs, three Junkers 88s approached from the north-west and dropped twenty (?) bombs, most 100 kilogram, from 2,000ft. One aircraft then turned and flew low over the Station with machine guns blazing but met with such a hot reception that it veered off to the north. This may have been the one which was afterwards brought down some 25 miles east-by-north of Linton. There were no casualties to personnel but a certain amount of damage was done to the aerodrome itself, the gas chamber was demolished and a few windows broken in the Transport Section.

Oberleutnant Friedrich-Franz Podbielski

After we had dropped our bombs, our starboard engine was hit and stopped. We lost height quickly and had to crash in a field behind a wood. We were quickly captured by armed civilians and then by

---

[3] He replaced *Oblt* Hajo Herrmann, later to become a highly decorated bomber and fighter pilot, who was injured in an accident on 18 October 1940.

police. The *Bordmechaniker Uffz* Otto Piontek was mortally injured in the crash and died that night. The same night I was taken by the police to York and interrogated.

Friedrich Podbielski's Ju 88 after its crash-landing. (via Cornwell)

Two more German bombers were lost during attacks on airfields on 27 October 1940 and a number damaged by ground fire; the effects of these attacks were negligible.[4] The remaining days of October 1940 were uneventful as far as the German bombers were concerned, the last loss being a Heinkel 111 of 9/KG 53 which became lost during an attack on Gravesend airfield on the night of 28/29 October, its crew all being taken prisoner. The Battle of Britain had ended but the battles over Britain had many more months and years to run.

Dornier 17Z of 5/KG 2 coded U5+AN which had taxied into a bomb crater at Cambrai–Sud after returning from an attack on London on the night of 27 October 1940; left to right Uffz Ernst Frohlich, Lt Karl Manowarda, Ofw *Helmut Petraschke,* Uffz Ernst Geselle.

[4] Some records state that *Oblt* Podbielski's Junkers 88 was shot down after attacking Driffield airfield but German records and Podbielski clearly state that Linton-on-Ouse was the target. It is therefore probable that *Oblt* Dietrich Marwitz, *Staffel Kapitaen* of 8/KG 30, was involved in the Driffield attack; he and his crew were reported to have been shot down by *Flak* and ditched off the Humber Estuary – there were no survivors.

Epilogue

1 November 1940 saw no real change in German tactics and air activity. A Dornier 17 of 4/KG 3 was apparently shot down by Hurricanes of 17 Squadron near a convoy sailing off the East Anglian coast. Spitfires of 64 Squadron then chased off an unidentified Heinkel 115 just before the fighter-bombers made their first appearance of the month over London. As this attack withdrew, a Messerschmitt 110 of 1(F)/22, probably assessing the effectiveness of the fighter-bomber attack, was damaged by Spitfires of 92 Squadron. For the next four hours, air activity was almost non-existent before a fighter sweep preceded an attack on a convoy off The Nore and shipping off Dover. The bombers in this case were Junkers 87 *Stukas* of StG 1, the *Stuka* being used offensively for the first time since 18 August 1940. They were heavily escorted and succeeded in sinking three ships for the loss of one *Stuka*. Then a few hours later, bombers and fighters of the *Regia Aeronautica* carried out an ineffectual foray over south-east Britain. The last daylight bomber incident occurred during the evening when a Junkers 88 of 8/KG 30 engaged on another attack on airfields in Yorkshire flew into a hillside near Whitby, killing all the crew. That night was a repeat of many previous nights with London, and this time Birmingham, receiving the attention of the German bombers. Two bombers fell victim to anti-aircraft fire.

A Stuka *of III/StG 1. The pilot who took this photo,* Oblt *Otto Blumers of 9/StG 1, was himself shot down and taken prisoner on 14 November 1940.* (Blumers)

Another casualty – this Do 17 of 1/KG 2 crash-landed at Vitry-en-Artois on returning from London on the night of 13 November 1940. (Hoehler)

The two months that followed the official Battle of Britain saw no let up in the German offensive, albeit daytime attacks by bombers, because of the painful lessons learned in the summer of 1940, had become few and far between. Bolstered by night time successes and fewer losses, the night offensive took precedence. However, on the night of 19/20 November 1940 a very significant combat took place when the first successful airborne radar-assisted night interception occurred; but at that time, the full significance was not apparent:

Night Combat Report for Flight Lieutenant John C Cunningham, 604 Squadron

> One aircraft, a 604 Squadron Beaufighter [callsign] non-Cockerel Blazer 24 (Flt Lt Cunningham), up 2221 hrs down 2259 hrs, engaged four-engined enemy aircraft type uncertain (Fw *Condor?*) near Brize Norton at 18,000ft at nearly same level and about 200 yards astern and at about same speed. Enemy aircraft returned fire almost immediately and appeared to slow down suddenly and turn to starboard. This enemy aircraft had no navigation lights and was intercepted by aid of: (a) Wallop control (b) Searchlight concentration on cloud (c) Airborne Interception (AI) Operator (d) Exhaust flames of enemy aircraft (e) Further instructions from AI Operator. Result inconclusive. Our casualties nil. Prior to this interception Blazer 24 sighted a smoke trail and two twin-engined enemy aircraft with navigation lights (believed formation of three twin-engined aircraft: six red lights were fired in pairs).

Later the following day, the wreckage of a Junkers 88 of 3/KG 54 was found at East Wittering in West Sussex; credit of its destruction went to John

'Cat's Eyes' Cunningham. It was the first of his twenty confirmed night kills and many hundreds more for the RAF's night fighter force.

The 'official' Battle of Britain is today recognised as being fought between 10 July and 31 October 1940. Nevertheless, this book has shown that the first major attack against Great Britain during World War Two by German bombers took place not on 10 July 1940 but some three weeks prior to that on the night of 18/19 June 1940. Furthermore, even though the 'official' Battle of Britain ended on 31 October 1940, the months that followed saw no let up in the *Luftwaffe*'s offensive, leading some historians to ask why we do not regard the Battle of Britain as ending on 18 May 1941 when the majority of German bomber and fighter units were withdrawn to the east for the invasion of the Soviet Union.

The night war was also intensifying for RAF Bomber Command and losses were increasing. Here Wellington T2501 of 99 Sqn shares Vitry-en-Artois airfield with a He 111 of KG 53 after force-landing on the night of 4 December 1940. (Hoehler)

It must be accepted that the 'official' Battle of Britain saw the fiercest air battles and greatest loss of life for both opposing air forces and if it were not for Fighter Command's men and women, the course of the war would have been totally different. Nevertheless, the battles over Britain continued for another four and a half years, not by day but the vast majority being at night. These battles could not be directly compared to those fought during the summer of 1940 but for those on the receiving end, they were just as dramatic as these final accounts show:

Combat Report for Pilot Officer Richard Stevens DFC, 151 Squadron

Plt Off Stevens, callsign Steeple 3, left RAF Wittering at 0032 hrs in a Hurricane with orders to orbit Coventry... At about 0140 hrs, he sighted another He 111 about 1,000ft above him also travelling westerly. He 'tailed' this and at about 200 yards range, the enemy started firing from the lower gun position. The Hurricane dived, came up underneath and fired a deflection burst from about 100 yards at nose and centre section. To evade the return fire from lower gun, he pulled up sharply on the port side and gave another burst upon which the enemy gunner ceased firing. The top gunner of the enemy aircraft was firing accurately and the Hurricane was hit several times. He then made another quarter attack from below and saw starboard motor on fire and leaving a stream of glycol which obscured his windscreen. He dropped back to wipe the windscreen with his glove and returned to the attack and noticed port motor on fire. A further burst from astern and below from 100 yards caused bits of enemy aircraft to fall away and then it dived steeply into a cloud layer. A further burst was fired and hit enemy aircraft which was not seen again although Plt Off Stevens followed it through the cloud. When last seen, both motors were on fire and inside the fuselage was also burning...[1]

Feldwebel Hans Kaufhold, 3/KG 55

On 9 April 1941 we took off from Le Bourget near Paris. It was my twenty-seventh operational flight. I had not flown during the summer of 1940 because I was recovering from wounds I received when I was shot down and taken prisoner on my fourteenth operational flight on 27 May 1940. I had started flying again on 28 November 1940 and had flown a number of night missions against Liverpool, London, Southampton, Glasgow, Bristol, Hull and Plymouth. Our target this night was Coventry.

Hans Kaufhold in the mid-upper position of a He 111. (Kaufhold)

[1] Richard Stevens was a successful single-seat night fighter pilot and had amassed fourteen and a half kills by the time of his death on 16 December 1941. It is possible that Sgt Alan Wagner and Sgt Stanislaw Seidengart flying a Defiant of 151 Squadron were also involved in this combat.

It was a clear night and the moon was shining. When we reached Portsmouth at a height of about 4,000m, we were shot at by *Flak*. Then, just over Coventry we were attacked by a Spitfire [sic]. The plane came out of the dark, the pilot must have seen us very well in the moonlight. He was in a good attacking position and during this attack, Herbert Link [the *Bordmechaniker*] was wounded in the upper arm.

After that, the Spitfire attacked from behind. Now it was my turn to shoot back. Everything happened so quickly and at that time I was not able to communicate with the rest of the crew as my intercom connection had been broken.

The Spitfire attacked again from where he had attacked first but, by that time, we could not fight back. Our plane was burning and in the meantime the bombs had been dropped. The last thing I heard was someone saying "Soellner! [*Ofw* Heinz Soellner, the pilot] At 1,000m there are some clouds so let's hide there!" After that, when I was watching the Spitfire, Herbert Link indicated that we should bale out – the order had come from the *Kommandeur* [*Hptm* Otto Bodemeyer, *Gruppen Kommandeur* of I/KG 55 and the *Beobachter*]. However, I misunderstood him and in the meantime, both in the cockpit jumped by parachute but we remained in the plane. Herbert had lost a lot of blood and was unconscious and we then were still in the plane when it crashed. I cannot describe what happened next

Hans Kaufhold (left) stands by the He 111 in which he was flying on 9 April 1941. (Kaufhold)

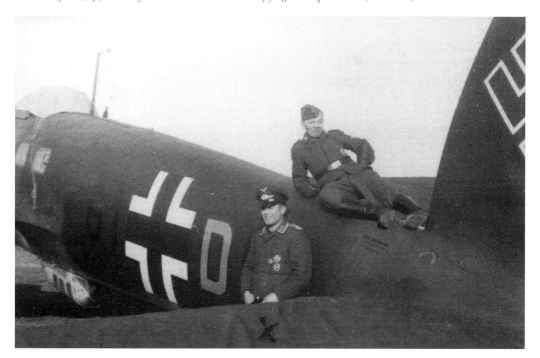

because I lost consciousness.

I think that when the plane hit the ground, both of us were catapulted out. When I regained consciousness, I was lying in a meadow with my flying suit on fire. I jumped to my feet and put out the flames but my wrists, hands and face had been burned. I hurried to get away from the plane – the ammunition was exploding and later, the fuel tanks exploded.

I followed a small path along to a road heard footsteps approaching and I hid behind a bush. When I eventually reached the road, I jumped into a ditch. I was in great pain from my burns and my lips had become very thick. I heard shouting and dogs barking – soldiers were looking for us German airmen but they failed to find me. I sat as still as a rabbit in the ditch and the seekers passed me by.

Soon the Fire Brigade came but there was little that they could do. It became quieter and soon there was nobody around. I wondered what to do – the road was empty so I came out of the

The same He 111 in pieces at a Leicestershire farm.

ditch and marched or should I say limped along the road. After a while, a car came around a bend and stopped in front of me. An RAF officer stepped out, raised his revolver and shouted "Hands up!" and so I was captured for the second and last time during the War.

For Hans Kaufhold, his war was finally over. For many more German bomber crews, the war would drag on and their suffering at the hands of the RAF would continue.

The scene at a German airfield at the end of the war – He 111s are broken up for scrap by the victorious Allies. (Camp)

Dramatis Personae

	Date	Unit	Aircraft	Crew	Fate
1.	19 June 1940	*Stab*/KG 4	He 111 H-4 2894 5J+GA	*Oblt* Heinz-Georg Corpus (*B, Adj*) – + *Lt* Erich Simon (*F*) – POW *Ofw* Walter Gross (*BM*) – + *Fw* Walter Wick (*BF*) – +	Shot down by Flt Lt A Malan, 74 Sqn and crashed at Bishop's Court Springfield Road, Writtle, Chelmsford, 0030 hrs
2.	19 June 1940	*Stab* II/KG 4	He 111 H-4 8747 5J+DM	*Maj* Dietrich Frhr Von Massenbach (*B, Gr Kdr*) – POW *Oblt* Ulrich Jordan (*F, TO*) – POW *Ofw* Max Leimer (*BF*) – POW *Fw* Karl Amberger (*BM*) – POW	Shot down by Flt Lt R Duke-Wooley/AC D Bell and Sgt A Close/LAC L Karasek of 23 Sqn and crashed at Blakeney Creek, Cley, Norfolk, 0045 hrs. Aircraft flown by Sgt Close also shot down in the combat
3.	19 June 1940	4/KG 4	He 111P-2 5J+AM	*Oblt* Joachim Von Arnim (*B*) – POW *Fw* Willi Maier (*F*) – POW *Fw* Karl Hauck (*BF*) – POW *Fw* Paul Gersch (*BM*) – +	Shot down by Sqn Ldr J O'Brien/Plt Off C King-Clark/Cpl D Little of 23 Sqn and Fg Off G W Petre of 19 Sqn and crashed at Six Mile Bottom, Great Wilbraham, Cambridgeshire, 0125 hrs; both RAF aircraft also shot down in the combat
4.	19 June 1940	6/KG 4	He 111 H 5J+FP	*Lt* Hansjuergen Backhaus (*F*) – POW *Fw* Alfred Reitzig (*B*) – + *Uffz* Theo Kuehn (*BF*) – POW *Uffz* Fritz Boeck (*BM*) – POW	Shot down by Fg Off G E Ball, 19 Sqn and ditched at Palm Bay, Margate, 0210 hrs
5.	1 July 1940	*Seenotflugkdo* 3	He 59 C-2 D-ASAM	*Lt* Hans-Joachim Fehske (*B*) – POW *Uffz* Ernst-Otto Nielsen (*F*) – POW *Gefr* Erich Philipp (*BF*) – POW *Uffz* Struckmann (*BM*) – POW	Shot down by Flt Lt E Graham, Fg Off E J Wilcox and Flt Sgt H Steere of 72 Sqn into the North Sea, 8 miles east of Sunderland, 0601 hrs

	Date	Unit	Aircraft	Crew	Fate
6.	1 July 1940	3/KG 4	He 111H-4 5J+EL	*Oblt* Friedrich-Wilhelm Koch (*B*) – POW *Ofw* Hermann Draisbach (*F*) – POW *Ofw* Rudolf Ernst (*BM*) – POW *Fw* Alfred Weber (*BF*) – POW	Shot down by Flt Lt R R Miller, Plt Off J Brewster and Plt Off J Bell of 616 Sqn into the sea off Hull, 1750 hrs
7.	12 July 1940	*Stab*/KG 55	He 111 P G1+FA	*Oblt* Walter Kleinhans (*B*) – + *Fw* John Moehn (*F*) – POW *Ofw* Fritz Knecht (*BM*) – POW *Ofw* Philipp Mueller (*BS*) – POW *Fw* Heinz Kalina (*BF*) – POW	Shot down by Sqn Ldr J Badger, Sgt C A Ayling, Plt Off H C Upton, Flt Lt T Dalton-Morgan, Plt Off D G Gorrie and Plt Off R A de Mancha of 43 Sqn and crash-landed at Hipley, Hampshire, 1430 hrs
8.	15 July 1940	2/KG 26	He 111 H-3 1H+EK	*Oblt* Ottmar Hollmann (*F*) – POW *Uffz* Erich Walz (*B*) – POW *Ogefr* Heinrich Probst (*BF*) – POW *Ogefr* Walter Reinhardt (*BM*) – + *Gefr* Josef Tretzger (*HS*) – POW	Shot down by Plt Off J S Morton and Plt Off D Stewart-Clarke of 603 Sqn and ditched 15 miles east of Peterhead, 1212 hrs
9.	21 July 1940	4(F)/14	Bf 110 C-5 2177 5F+CM	*Oblt* Friedrich-Karl Runde (*F*) – POW *Fw* Willi Baden (*BF*) – POW	Shot down by Flt Lt D E Turner, Plt Off C T Davis and Plt Off J Wigglesworth, 238 Sqn and crash-landed at Home Farm, Goodwood, West Sussex, 1020 hrs
10.	21 July 1940	4(F)/14	Do 17 M-1 5F+OM	*Lt* Georg Thiel (*B*) – POW *Fw* Fritz Bohnen (*F*) – POW *Uffz* Alfred Werner (*BF*) – POW	Shot down by Sqn Ldr H A Fenton, Flt Lt D E Turner, Plt Off J S Wigglesworth, Fg Off C T Davis and Sgt L G Batt of 238 Sqn and crash-landed at Nutford Farm, Blandford, Dorset, 1445 hrs
11.	24 July 1940	2/KG 40	FW 200 C F8+BH	*Hptm* Volkmar Zenker (*F*) – POW *Fw* Willi Andreas (*BM*) – + *Uffz* Rudolf Wagner (*F*) – + *Uffz* Heinz Hoecker (*BF*) – POW *Gefr* Leo Hohmann (*BS*) – POW	Suffered engine failure and ditched 15 miles north-east of Belfast, 0340 hrs

12. 8 August 1940	8/StG 1	Ju 87 B J9+GK	*Oblt* Klaus Ostmann (*F*) – W *Ofw* Wuestner (*BF*) – uninj	Possibly damaged by Sqn Ldr J R A Peel, 145 Sqn; landed at Theville with 60 percent damage
13. 8 August 1940	*Stab* II/StG 77	Ju 87 B	*Hptm* Waldemar Plewig (*F, Gr Kdr*) – POW *Fw* Kurt Schauer (*BF*) – +	Shot down off the Isle of Wight, 1720 hrs
14. 12 August 1940	*Stab*/KG 51	Ju 88 A-1 9K+AA	*Oberst Dr* Hans Fisser (*Gesch Komm*) – + *Oblt* Werner Luederitz (*F*) – POW *Lt* Franz Schad (*B*) – POW *Sd Fhr* Adam Nothelfer – POW	Shot down by a number of pilots including Sgt E Shepperd, 152 Sqn and crash-landed at Godshill Park, Isle of Wight, 1230 hrs
15. 12 August 1940	3/KG 51	Ju 88 A-1 9K+CL	*Uffz* Karl Zimmermann (*F*) – POW *Ogefr* Karl-Heinz Fahrenheim (*BM*) – POW *Ogefr* Oskar Hansmann (*BF*) – POW *Gefr* Theodor Dickel (*B*) – +	Shot down by fighters and crashed into the Solent, 1220 hrs
16. 12 August 1940	8/KG 51	Ju 88A-1 4078 9K+BS	*Oblt* Eberhard Wildermuth (*F*) – POW *Oblt* Otto Staerk (*B*) – POW *Uffz* Heinz Droese (*BF*) – POW *Uffz* Konrad Roesch (*BM*) – +	Tail shot off by AA fire and crashed into Portsmouth Harbour, 1230 hrs
17. 13 August 1940	*Stab*/KG 2	Do 17Z U5+KA	*Oblt* Heinz Schlegel (*F*) – POW *Oblt* Gerhard Osswald (*B, St Kap*) – POW *Ofw* Gustav Babbe (*BF*) – POW *Ofw* Ernst Holz (*B*) – POW	Possibly shot down by Plt Off J A Walker of 111 Sqn; crashed at Pherbec Bridge, Barham, Kent, 0830 hrs
18. 15 August 1940	10 (*Stuka*)/LG1	Ju 87 B	*Hptm* Rolf Muenchenhagen (*F*) – POW *Fw* Herbert Heise (*BF*) – +	Shot down by Hurricanes of 501 Sqn into the sea off Folkestone, 1140 hrs

No.	Date	Unit	Aircraft	Crew	Fate
19.	15 August 1940	8/KG 26	He 111 H-4 1H+FS	*Oblt* Hermann Riedel (*F*) – uninj *Ofw* Paul Suessenbach (*BF*) – uninj *Ofw* Kalle Mueller (*BM*) – uninj *Fw* Willi Scholl (*B*) – uninj	Shot down into the North Sea, c.1300 hrs
20.	15 August 1940	1/KG 26	He 111 H-4 1H+GH	*Oblt* Rudolf Roch (*B*) – POW *Uffz* Willi Zimmermann (*F*) – POW *Gefr* Erwin Kulick (*BF*) – POW *Gefr* Alwin Machalett (*BM*) – POW *Flg* Ernst Henrichsen (*HS*) – POW	Believed to have been shot down by Plt Off W Millington, 79 Sqn and ditched in Cresswell Bay, Blyth, 1300 hrs
21.	15 August 1940	7/KG 30	Ju 88 A-4 5648 4D+DR	*Oblt* Werner Bachmann (*F*) – POW *Fw* Georg Henneske (*BF*) – + *Uffz* Werner Evers (*B*) – POW *Flg* Robert Walther (*BM*) – POW	Shot down by Spitfire of 616 Sqn and crashed at Hornby near Bridlington, 1325 hrs
22.	15 August 1940	4/LG 1	Ju 88 A-1 L1+FM	*Uffz* Fritz Dieter (*F*) – POW *Uffz* Willi Rimek (*B*) – + *Uffz* Otto Rezeppa (*BF*) – POW *Gefr* Werner Hohbom (*BM*) – POW	Shot down by Flt Lt S D P Connors of 111 Sqn and crash-landed at Great Ham Farm, Earnley, West Sussex, 1830 hrs
23.	15 August 1940	*Stab* II/LG 1	Ju 88 A-1 L1+SC	*Oblt* Stephan Suin de Boutemard (*F*) – POW *Ofw* Heinz Grund (*B*) – POW *Fw* Kurt Weigang (*BF*) – POW *Fw* Willi Lueder (*BM*) – POW	Shot down by Flt Lt A Hope and Sgt L Guy of 601 Sqn and crash-landed at The Jumps, West Tisted, Hampshire, 1810 hrs
24.	15 August 1940	*Seenotstaffel* IV	He 59 C D-AFFK	*Lt zS* Siegfried Boerner (*B*) – + Rest of crew and crew of *Oblt* Riedel of 8/KG 26 uninj	Shot down by a Hudson of 206 Sqn into the North Sea, 2230 hrs
25.	16 August 1940	3/StG 2	Ju 87 B-1	*Uffz* Ernst Koenig (*F*) – POW *Uffz* Josef Schmid (*BF*) – POW	Shot down by fighters into the sea south of Selsey Bill, 1400 hrs

26. 18 August 1940	6/KG 76	Ju 88 A-1 F1+GP	*Fw* Karl Krebs (*F*) – + *Fw* Otto Watermann (*BF*) – POW *Uffz* Horst Loeffler (*BS*) – POW *Sd Fhr* Willi Perchemeier – POW	Probably shot down by Sgt P C P Farnes of 501 Sqn and crashed at Aylesford near West Malling, Kent, 1340 hrs
27. 21 August 1940	2/KG 2	Do 17 Z-3 U5+FK	*Lt* Heinz Ermecke (*F*) – + *Uffz* Goetz-Dieter Wolf (*B*) – POW *Uffz* Heinz Hermsen (*BF*) – POW *Sd Fhr* Kurt Rasche – POW	Shot down by Flt Lt G Powell-Sheddon, Sub Lt R E Gardner and Plt Off J B Latta of 242 Sqn and crashed at Conifer Hill, Starston, Norfolk, 1252 hrs
28. 21 August 1940	6/KG 3	Do 17Z-3 5K+AP	*Oblt* Herbert Schwartz (*F, St Kap*) – POW *Oblt* Ulrich Matschoss (*B*) – POW *Ofw* Wilhelm Loos (*BF*) – + *Uffz* Helmut Lehmann (*BF*) – +	Damaged by Sqn Ldr J McComb, Sgt A D Burt and Sgt A S Darling of 611 Sqn and then collided in cloud with Do 17 flown by *Uffz* Georg Pollmann of 6/KG 3; crashed at Alford, Lincolnshire, 1314 hrs
29. 21 August 1940	4/KG 54	Ju 88 A-1 B3+BM	*Hptm* Lothar Maiwald (*B, St Kap*) – POW *Ofw* Heinz Apollony (*F*) – POW *Uffz* Kurt Miethner (*BF*) – POW *Uffz* Helmut Hempel (*BM*) – POW	Shot down by Sqn Ldr C Williams, Plt Off H A Bird-Williams and Plt Off J Ross of 17 Sqn and crash-landed at Marsh Farm, Earnley, West Sussex, 1615 hrs
30. 23 August 1940	*Stab*/KG 2	Do 17 Z U5+EA	*Oblt* Joachim-Heinrich Hellmers (*B, St Kap*) – POW *Ofw* Guenther Wagner (*F*) – POW *Fw* Albert Dietel (*BF*) – POW *Uffz* Paul Seidel (*BM*) – POW	Damaged by AA fire and crash-landed at Lodge Farm, Wickhambrook, Suffolk, 0920 hrs
31. 28 August 1940	6/KG 3	Do 17 Z-3 4251 5K+LP	*Lt* Peter Krug (*F, St Fhr*) – POW *Gefr* Artur Burghardt (*B*) – POW *Gefr* Willi Gailer (*BF*) – POW *Flg* Anton Brueckmann (*BS*) – POW	Damaged by AA fire and then shot down by Sqn Ldr J Leathart, 54 Sqn off Palm Bay, Margate, 1245 hrs

No.	Date	Unit	Aircraft / Serial / Code	Crew	Fate
32.	30 August 1940	7/KG 53	He 111 H-2 2624 A1+CR	*Lt* Ernst Fischbach (*F*) – POW *Fw* Wilhelm Kusserow (*B*) – POW *Fw* Georg Distler (*BF*) – POW *Gefr* Leo Stilp (*HS*) – + *Gefr* Walter Reis (*HS*) – +	Shot down by Flt Lt W Rhodes-Moorhouse, Plt Off H T Gilbert, Sgt N Taylor and Fg Off T Grier of 601 Sqn and crashed at The Rectory, Hunsdon, Hertfordshire, 1630 hrs
33.	30 August 1940	3/KG 53	He 111 H-2 5532 A1+IL	*Lt* Wulff Roessler (*B*) – POW *Uffz* Helmut Gall (*F*) – POW *Uffz* Ernst-Erhard von Kuehnheim (*BF*) – + *Uffz* Adolf Saam (*BM*) – + *Ogefr* Otto Fischer (*BS*) – +	Shot down by Sgt H J Merchant of 1 Sqn and crashed at Lifstan Way, Southend, Essex, 1715 hrs
34.	31 August 1940	2/KG 76	Do 17 Z 3316 F1+BK	*Lt* Josef Kleppmeier (*F*) – POW *Ofw* Heinrich Lang (*BM*) – POW *Fw* Harald Pfaehler (*B*) – POW *Uffz* Albert Bloss (*BF*) – POW	Damaged by AA fire and probably damaged further by Sgt M H Pocock of 72 Sqn and crash-landed at Newchurch, East Sussex, 1800 hrs
35.	5 September 1940	*Stab* I/KG 1	He 111 H-3 3324 V4+AB	*Maj* Ludwig Maier (*Gr Kdr*) – + *Oblt* Peter Biebrach (*F, TO*) – POW *Oblt* Graf Job-Wilhelm von Rittberg (*B*) – + *Ofw* Erwin Stockert (*BF*) – + *Uffz* Horst Bendig (*BM*) – +	Shot down by Plt Off M J Herrick/Sgt J S Pugh of 25 Sqn and crashed at Rendlesham, Suffolk, 0110 hrs
36.	9 September 1940	*Stab* III/KG 53	He 111 H-2 2630 A1+ZD	*Oblt* Kurt Meinecke (*B*) – POW *Ofw* Oskar Broderix (*F*) – POW *Fw* Ernst Wendorff (*BF*) – + *Fw* Wilhelm Wenninger (*BM*) – + *Fw* Willi Doering (*BS*) – +	Collided with Hurricane flown by Plt Off G M Forrester of 605 Sqn and crashed at Southfield Farm, Chawton, Hampshire, 1800 hrs

No.	Date / Unit	Aircraft	Code	Crew	Remarks
37.	11 September 1940 *Stab* II/KG 26	He 111H-3 6856	1H+AC	*Maj* Eckhard Christian (*Gr Kdr*) – uninj / *Fw* Krothe (*F*) – uninj / *Ofw* Ziermann (*BF*) – uninj / *Fw* Richard Herrmann (*BM*) – W / *Gefr* Wilhelm Zimmer (*B*) – uninj	Damaged in combat
38.	11 September 1940 1/KG 26	He 111 H 6962	1H+AH	*Hptm* Wolfgang Kuenstler (*F, St Kap*) – POW / *Fw* Erich Buettner (*F*) – POW / *Fw* Johannes Schaefer (*BF*) – + / *Uffz* Walter Schang (*B*) – + / *Uffz* Erich Schmidt (*BM*) – POW	Believed shot down by Plt Off E S Lock of 41 Sqn and crashed at Cripps Corner, Sedlescombe, 1630 hrs
39.	13 September 1940 8/KG 27	He 111P 2670	1G+DS	*Oblt* Harry Wappler (*F*) – POW / *Ofw* Johannes Elster (*BF*) – + / *Uffz* Fritz Bernd (*B*) – + / *Uffz* Herbert Okuneck (*BM*) – +	Collided with barrage balloon cable and crashed at 32 Stow Park Avenue, Newport, Monmouthshire, 0330 hrs
40.	14 September 1940 3/KG 4	He 111 H-4 3294	5J+BL	*Oblt* Hermann Kell (*F, St Fhr*) – POW / *Fw* Walter Hobe (*B*) – POW / *Ogefr* Werner Mueller-Wernscheidt (*BF*) – + / *Uffz* Hermann Toepfer (*BM*) – +	Shot down by Plt Off M J Herrick/Plt Off A Brown of 25 Sqn and crashed at Newmans End, Sheering, Essex, 0155 hrs
41.	15 September 1940 8/KG 76	Do 17 Z 2555	F1+FS	*Fw* Rolf Heitsch (*F*) – POW / *Fw* Stephan Schmid (*BF*) – + / *Fw* Hans Pfeiffer (*B*) – POW / *Fw* Martin Sauter (*BM*) – POW	Shot down by Fg Off J Dundas and Plt Off E Tobin of 609 Sqn and crash-landed at Castle Farm, Shoreham, Kent, 1210 hrs
42.	16 September 1940 3/506	He 115 C 3261	S4+CL	*Hptm* Ernst-Wilhelm Bergemann (*St Kap*) – POW / *Hptm* Hans Kriependorf (*B*) – POW / *Lt* Clemens Lucas (*F*) – POW / *Fw* Erich Kalinowski (*BF*) – POW	Damaged by AA fire and ditched in North Sea 7.5 miles north-east of Eyemouth, 0035 hrs

No.	Date / Unit	Aircraft / Serial / Code	Crew	Circumstances
43.	16 September 1940 1/906	He 115 C-1 2754 8L+GH	Hptm Heinrich Kothe (F) – POW Lt zS Hans-Otto Aldus (B) – POW Uffz Herbert Meissner (BF) – POW	Became lost in poor weather and hit hillside at Rosehearty, Fraserburgh, 2200 hrs
44.	21 September 1940 *Aufkl.ObdL*	Do 215 B 0023 VB+KK	Lt Rolf Book (B) – POW Fw Kurt Jensen (F) – POW Fw Hans Kuehl (BF) – POW Uffz Gustav Pelzer (BM) – +	Shot down by Plt Off D Adams of 611 Sqn and crashed at Trawsfynydd, Merioneth, 1655 hrs
45.	25 September 1940 1/KG 55	He 111H 6305 G1+BH	Hptm Karl Koethke (B) – POW Fw Fritz Juerges (F) – POW Uffz Rudolf Weisbach (BF) – POW Uffz Otto Mueller (BS) – POW Uffz Josef Altrichter (BM) – +	Shot down by Plt Off J S Wigglesworth of 238 Sqn and Plt Off J Curchin of 609 Sqn and crash-landed at Westhill Farm, Studland, Dorset, 1200 hrs
46.	30 September 1940 2/KG 77	Ju 88 A-1 2142 3Z+DK	Oblt Friedrich Oeser (F) – POW Ofw Gustav Gorke (BF) – POW Uffz Georg Klasing (BM) – + Gefr Rudi Hulsmann (BS) – POW	Shot down by Sgt P C Farnes of 501 Sqn and crash-landed on Gatwick Race Course, 1500 hrs
47.	2 October 1940 *Stab*/KG 2	Do 17 Z 3423 U5+FA	Oblt Hans Langer (F, *St Kap*) – POW Oblt Erich Eitze (B) – POW Uffz Robert Seidel (BF) – POW Uffz Helmut Bellmann (BM) – POW	Shot down by Flt Lt A W A Bayne, Plt Off F Fajtl, Fg Off H P Blatchford, Plt Off J K Ross and Plt Off L W Stevens of 17 Sqn and crash-landed at Rookery Farm, Cretingham, Suffolk, 1020 hrs
48.	7 October 1940 5/KG 51	Ju 88 A-1 8064 9K+SN	Oblt Sigurd Hey (F) – POW Lt Fritz Bein (B) – POW Ofw Christian Koenig (BF) – POW Ofw Josef Krell (BM) – POW	Shot down by a number of fighters including Plt Off R F T Doe of 238 Sqn and Sgt E E Shepperd of 152 Sqn and crashed at Sydling St Nicholas, Dorset, 1630 hrs
49.	11 October 1940 1/606	Do 17 Z-3 2772 7T+EH	Lt zS Juergen von Krause (B) – POW Fw Josef Vetterl (F) – + Fw Heinrich Arpert (BM) – POW Ogefr Helmut Sundermann (BF) – POW	Shot down by Fg Off D H Watkins and Plt Off T Draper Williams of 611 Sqn and ditched off Bardsey Islands, 1830 hrs

50. 25 October 1940	2(F)/122	Bf 110 C 2257 F6+MK	*Lt* Konrad Wacker (*F*) – POW *Gefr* Heinrich Gneist (*BF*) – +	Shot down by Plt Off N R Norfolk, Sgt M Pocock and Sgt J White of 72 Sqn and crashed in the sea off Yarmouth, 1440 hrs
51. 27 October 1940	7/KG 30	Ju 88 A-5 6129 5J+ER	*Oblt* Friedrich-Franz Podbielski (*F, St Fhr*) – POW *Ofw* Karl von Kiedrowski (*BF*) – POW *Fw* Heinz Heier (*B*) – POW *Uffz* Oskar Piontek (*BS*) – +	Damaged by AA fire and crash-landed at Richmond Farm, Duggleby, Yorkshire, 1800 hrs
52. 9 April 1941	3/KG 55	He 111 P-4 2962 G1+DL	*Hptm* Otto Bodemeyer (*B, Gr Kdr*) – POW *Ofw* Heinz Soellner (*F*) – POW *Fw* Hans Kaufhold (*BF*) – POW *Fw* Herbert Link (*BM*) – POW	Shot down by Plt Off R P Stevens of 151 Sqn and crashed at Roes Rest Farm between Desford and Peckleton, Leicestershire, 0145 hrs

Select Bibliography

Balke, Ulf, *Der Luftkrieg in Europa 1939-41*, Bechtermuenz Verlag, Augsburg, 1997

Caldwell, Donald, *The JG 26 War Diary, Volume 1, 1939-42*, Grub Street, London, 1996

Collier, Richard, *Eagle Day*, Pan Books, London, 1968

Dierich, Wolfgang, *Kampfgeschwader 55 'Greif'*, Motorbuchverlag, Stuttgart, 1975

Dierich, Wolfgang, *Kampfgeschwader Edelweiss*, Ian Allan, Shepperton, 1975

Foreman, John, *Battle of Britain – The Forgotten Months*, Air Research Publications, Walton on Thames, 1988

Foreman, John, *Fighter Command War Diary Part 1*, Air Research Publications, Walton on Thames, 1996

Foreman, John, *Fighter Command War Diary Part 2*, Air Research Publications, Walton on Thames, 1998

Goss, Christopher, *Brothers in Arms*, Crécy Books, Bristol, 1994

Mason, Francis, *Battle over Britain*, McWhirter Twins, London, 1969

Norman, Bill, *Luftwaffe over the North*, Leo Cooper, London, 1993

Patzwall, Klaus, *Luftwaffe Rangliste 1945*, Militaer Verlag Klaus D Patzwall, Norderstedt, 1986

Price, Alfred, *The Hardest Day*, Macdonald & James, London, 1979

Price, Dr Alfred, *Battle of Britain Day 15 September 1940*, The RAF Air Power Review, Volume 2 No 2

Ramsey, Winston (Ed.), *The Battle of Britain Then and Now Mark III*, Battle of Britain Prints, London, 1985

Shores, Christopher & Williams, Clive, *Aces High*, Grub Street, London, 1994

Vasco, John, *Bombsights over England*, JAC Publications, Norwich, 1990

Wakefield, Ken, *The First Pathfinders*, Crécy Books, Bristol, 1992

Wynn, Kenneth, *Men of the Battle of Britain*, Gliddon Books, Norwich, 1989

Index